# FORTRESS EUROPE'S INNER WALL

## Migrant Dilemmas at the Brenner Pass

MARCO FUNK

# Contents

Introduction ...................................................................................1

**Part 1: First Encounters at the Brenner**..........................................5

Day One...........................................................................................5

The North Pole's unexpected visitors ......................................... 13

Switzerland's unwanted economist............................................. 19

Stranded Somalis .......................................................................... 26

Desperate souls in a desperate country ....................................... 29

**Part 2: Stories from Europe's Purgatory** ..................................... 33

African predicaments and European failures .............................. 33

Opportunists, smugglers and undocumented tourists............... 41

Fleeing Boko Haram, Libyan prisons and Sicilian reception
centres ........................................................................................... 45

Italy's migrant dilemma ............................................................... 49

Local reactions: solidarity, protest and deception...................... 54

The Italian migrant who changed his mind about migrants ..... 57

The witch doctor's sacrifice and other stories............................. 59

**Part 3: Sicily, the Gateway to Europe**.......................................... 67

Palermo .......................................................................................... 68

Reception hell and heaven in Salemi ........................................... 70

Siculiana and Porto Empedocle ................................................... 74

Friendly nuns and hungry refugees in Agrigento....................... 77

Caltanissetta's Pakistani community............................................ 80

Mineo, Europe's largest refugee business.................................... 83

Pozzallo, Syracuse and Augusta ................................................. 88

The Angels of Catania........................................................................92

Akil's perilous journey from Syria to Sicily ....................................99

From Milan to the Inner Wall........................................................104

**Part 4: Politics, Paradoxes and Solutions**................................107

The besieged Inner Wall.................................................................107

The consequences of closed borders............................................110

Fallacies and false assumptions....................................................116

Trickery in Dublin's shadow..........................................................121

Answers to northern European concerns ....................................126

Unfounded fears and unrecognised opportunities ....................130

Public opinion: the key to better migration policies.................135

Europe's forgotten legacy...............................................................138

**Acknowledgements** ........................................................................140

**About the Author**...........................................................................142

# Introduction

The media has used the term "Fortress Europe" in recent years to describe the European Union's increasingly closed-door policy towards migrants attempting to reach Europe from Africa and the Middle East. The metaphor mainly refers to the EU's external borders, especially its southern ones: the Mediterranean coasts of Italy, Greece and Spain. Like a moat surrounding a medieval fortress, the Mediterranean Sea acts as a barrier against unwanted intruders. The island of Lampedusa, an Italian outpost in the moat, became a symbol of the humanitarian cost of this first line of defence after a shipwreck killed over 350 migrants just off the island's coast in October 2013. Italy responded with its "Mare Nostrum" search and rescue operation, which ran until the end of October 2014.

Over 100,000 refugees arrived in Sicily in this period, in addition to those who had arrived before. Many didn't want to stay in Italy, due to family ties or friends in other European countries, language abilities and/or employment opportunities, and an increasing number wanted to leave due to steadily deteriorating reception conditions. But Europe's asylum system trapped them in Italy. The EU's so-called Dublin Regulation, which is also applied by Switzerland, Liechtenstein, Norway and Iceland, states that an asylum application must be handled by the first member state that a refugee enters, with very few exceptions.

The financial and political cost of saving migrants' lives while overburdening local communities led to the replacement of Mare Nostrum with Operation Triton, an EU-led border control mission. In contrast to Mare Nostrum, which stretched far south into the Mediterranean Sea, Triton was initially limited to 30 nautical miles (approximately 55 km) from shore and was not primarily intended to save lives. Search and rescue efforts were only restored to previous levels after a series of tragedies made the human cost of Europe's moat grotesquely visible. At the same time, a second natural line of defence against the defenceless, Italy's Alpine border with its northern neighbours – Fortress Europe's Inner Wall – was reinforced.

This book is about one of the few, and one of the most important gateways to the other side of the Inner Wall: the Brenner Pass. At 1,370 metres above sea level in the middle of the Alps, it is the lowest and most important mountain pass connecting Italy, Austria and Germany by road and rail. It is also the border between Italy and Austria, marking the northernmost limit that boat migrants are allowed to go in pursuit of a better life. But the EU's asylum laws don't mean much to those who have risked their lives crossing deserts and seas to escape war and poverty.

Thousands of refugees have attempted to reach northern Europe via the Brenner in recent years, and the Austrian and German authorities have taken notice. In an effort to counteract the influx of migrants, Austrian police increasingly boarded international trains from Verona to Munich at the Brenner to check passengers' documents, identify irregular migrants and make them get off the train in Innsbruck, the next city along the route. Due to a bilateral agreement with Italy dating back to 1997, Austria is authorized to return travellers coming from Italy who cannot provide documentation valid for a legal stay in Austria. According to Italian police figures, over 5,000 returns of this sort were carried out by the Austrian police in 2014.

Police checks intensified in November 2014, when daily joint patrols with Austrian, German and Italian officers on international trains began. In order to catch irregular migrants before they even enter Austria, police board trains in Trento, 140 km south of the border, in order to kick migrants off the trains in Bolzano, the next city further north, or latest at the Brenner. Practically all migrants continue their journey after this initial setback, taking regional trains to the Brenner. Once they reach it, they find themselves in a remote Alpine village, literally a few steps away from the promised North, but are not allowed to reach it.

Many refugees who arrive at the Brenner are not prepared for the unexpected stop high up in the mountains. Some come straight from Sicily, having crossed the Mediterranean only a few days before. In order to provide basic humanitarian support to those stranded at the border, Volontarius, a local NGO, was commissioned by the government of South Tyrol, the bilingual Italian-German province of Italy bordering

Austria, to maintain a presence at Brenner train station, which is located on the Italian side of the border. Volunteers and social workers started providing food, drinks, clothing, basic medical attention, information and general assistance to migrants who ended up there in late December 2014.

I decided to start volunteering at the Brenner in January 2015. I had worked for the International Organization for Migration (IOM) in Vienna the year before, where I gained an understanding of Austrian and EU migration laws in theory, but wanted to see what things looked like in practice. I was especially interested in the Brenner due to its geographic location, political significance and the absurdity of an Alpine village becoming a purgatory for migrants in limbo.

This book describes my experiences with migrants I've met at the Brenner while working as a volunteer, as well as the political context of their journeys. It also presents my observations and reflections from a trip to Sicily, which I undertook in order to better understand why so many refugees leave the island in order to reach northern Europe. In the interest of privacy, the names of the people I've met have been changed, but I have made every effort to tell their stories and recount my observations accurately.

# Part 1: First Encounters at the Brenner

## Day One

My first day volunteering at the Brenner started on a cold, sunny morning in late January 2015. As I approached Fortress Europe's Inner Wall on the train from my home town to the south, I thought of what it must feel like for an African refugee to see such a seemingly inhospitable landscape of mountains and snow for the first time. The closer the train got to the Brenner, the taller the peaks, the thicker the layer of snow covering everything, and the colder it looked outside. The train snaked its way up the narrowing valley, and finally reached the end of the line: Brennero/Brenner.

I stepped outside into the frigid air, which was forecasted to reach a maximum of -6°C that day, and walked along the platform to an underpass which led to the other platforms and the station's entrance. I had taken an Italian regional train from Bolzano, and its arrival coincided with the departure of an Austrian regional train to Innsbruck. All of my fellow passengers walked over to the platform where the train to Innsbruck was waiting. The train left, and I was practically alone at the station. Only a man emptying rubbish bins was to be seen on one of the platforms.

I made a few rounds searching for other volunteers and finally spotted a blonde girl and a tall young man standing in front of a ticket machine with two Africans.

I introduced myself, and sure enough, they were who I was looking for: Giovanna, who was doing a year of Italian civilian service before starting university, and Carlos, a Spaniard who had completed his Bachelor's degree and was spending a year abroad doing European Voluntary Service before continuing his studies. They were helping the two Africans try to retrieve a 50 Euro note that the ticket machine took without printing tickets.

The Brenner train station doesn't have a staffed ticket counter, so Giovanna went to look for someone who could help us get the money back. The only train company employees she could find were two workers in charge of managing the rail network in an office marked with a "No Entry" sign, who were in no mood to help. After Giovanna convinced them to make a phone call, they informed her that a complaint had to be filed in person at the ticket counter in Vipiteno or Bressanone, the next larger towns down the valley further south. The money could only be refunded after the complaint was processed and it was verified that the machine had indeed taken the banknote without printing a ticket.

Giovanna returned with the bad news as we were still standing in front of the machine, hoping it would spit out the money. We decided to wait a little longer, just in case, and I struck up a conversation with the unlucky young men. They were from Gambia, the smallest state on the African continent – a sliver of land in West Africa surrounded on all sides by Senegal, except for a short coastline on the Atlantic Ocean.

The more talkative one, Lamin, explained that he arrived in Sicily in June of last year and spent almost seven months in a small town near Palermo. He didn't know whether he would receive a residence permit, and didn't get any help from the owner of the house he stayed in. He tried to deal with the police directly, but every time he went to the local Questura, Italy's provincial police authority in charge of immigration, he was turned away and told to come back "domani" – tomorrow. Frustrated by this – in his own words – "African mentality", he decided to head to Germany with Robert, the less talkative one. Lamin had heard from another migrant he befriended in Sicily who had since made it to Munich that things were better organized in Germany.

The two of them left Palermo on a train to Rome, then travelled on to Milan, and proceeded to reach Munich via the Brenner. They made it all the way to Innsbruck, but were caught by the Austrian police, brought back to the Brenner in a police van, and handed over to the Italian authorities. Their fingerprints were taken, but the Italian police assured them that they were only checking whether they had a criminal record – not using the fingerprints for immigration purposes. In other words, their fingerprints wouldn't be entered in the Europe-wide EURODAC database of irregular migrants, which would provide clear proof of Italy's responsibility for them under the Dublin Regulation.

They were both given a document requesting them to appear at the Questura in Bolzano the following day in order to regularize their status in Italy, but after being given this document, the police told them that they should rip it up if they decided to try reaching Germany again. As an added encouragement, they were advised to avoid taking any direct train to Munich before the last one of the day, which would leave the Brenner at 20:00 and which wouldn't be checked by police.

Lamin and Robert wanted to save time by taking the regional train to Innsbruck and a train to Germany from there, but faced with the loss of 50 Euros, they decided to wait all day for the last train to Munich. Giovanna, Carlos and I brought them to the waiting room and promised to return with scarves and gloves, since the barren room was barely heated. Before heading to a flat that Volontarius had rented in the village to serve as a storage space for donations and a home base for volunteers, we waited for the 12 o'clock international train to arrive in order to see whether anyone was kicked off and in need of assistance.

EuroCity 88 arrived on time and sure enough, a black teenager, aged 16 at most, was escorted off the train by three police officers. Their uniforms confirmed that it was the tri-national patrol: Italian POLIZIA, Austrian POLIZEI and German POLIZEI. The teenager was alone, and was taken to the Brenner's police station with his head hanging low. No one else got off the train, so we headed to the flat to get the scarves and gloves and eat lunch.

The NGO's flat was a three minute walk from the station, as pretty much everything else in the village. It consisted of a small kitchen, a bathroom and a large living room with a wooden table and typical Tyrolean corner bench, some old couches and several tall shelves on the walls stuffed with donated clothing and shoes. We looked for scarves and gloves that would fit Lamin and Robert, and brought the winter gear plus a canister of hot tea and a bag full of sandwiches back out to the station. The next train to Munich was already there when we arrived, but we didn't see anyone on the platform except for a few smokers taking advantage of the break.

We walked over to the waiting room and stepped inside. Lamin and Robert were still there, but they were now in the company of another African who appeared to be in his mid to late twenties. He introduced himself as Kibrom, from Eritrea, a small East African country on the Red Sea. Unlike Lamin and Robert, who appeared well-rested and were well groomed, Kibrom looked tired and slightly dishevelled. Nevertheless, he had the air of an intellectual; he was soft spoken and crossed his legs elegantly while sitting, the same way politicians do when they're on television talk shows.

Kibrom had arrived in Sicily barely a week before reaching the Brenner, which explained his visible fatigue. Like Lamin and Robert, he wanted to reach a friend in Germany. Before crossing the Mediterranean, he spent over a year in Libya trying to earn enough money to pay for the crossing. However, what he experienced there sounded like hell on earth.

Lamin and Robert also spent a few months in Libya, and the three of them explained that the country is in a state of anarchy fuelled by guns and cheap petrol. Practically all the Libyans they met were armed and owned a car, but didn't appear to have a job. Libyans would often rob migrants at gunpoint, and shoot them if they had no money to offer – even a single dinar could make the difference between life and death. The police not only turned a blind eye, but was even more dangerous than thieves. Migrants were often arrested for no reason and packed into overcrowded prisons; in order to be released, they had to pay a ransom, or if they had no money, ask friends or family members back home to transfer the amount. Kibrom spent two months in prison, but managed to escape with a few others by digging a small tunnel under the prison wall.

Lamin, who was accompanied by his uncle, managed to avoid prison by staying in a safe house practically all the time and guarding the money they brought to pay a "businessman" for the Mediterranean crossing. The two of them ended up on two different boats and sadly, his uncle drowned when his boat sank. Lamin was lucky; his boat was intercepted by the Italian Coast Guard, which brought him to safety.

In order to pay for the crossing, Kibrom had to find work as a day labourer in Libya, which often meant a day of heavy physical labour and no pay at the end. Those who protested were usually threatened at gunpoint. Despite the odds, Kibrom managed not only to earn enough money to pay a smuggler, but was also clever enough to hide it from thieves. Hiding money well was essential due to the frequent robberies, and he proudly explained that he hid his money in places the Libyans wouldn't look: in his underwear and in the soles of his shoes.

I asked them whether they knew about all these risks when they started their trip, and they said they did, but decided to try their luck anyway. Stories of people who had made it to Europe were as plenty as stories of those who had died trying, and according to them, the attempt was worth the risks. Life at home was simply too miserable to forego the chance of a better life in Europe. Lamin and Robert lamented the undemocratic government and lack of jobs in Gambia, while Kibrom fled compulsory military service in Eritrea, which is akin to life in a gulag.

At around four o'clock, the next train to Munich arrived. Giovanna, Carlos and I stepped out on the platform, which was absolutely frigid now that the sun had already disappeared behind the mountains. No one was kicked off, so Giovanna and Carlos decided to call it a day and we planned to take the next regional train back home. We said goodbye to Lamin, Robert and Kibrom, leaving them a bag full of sandwiches and wishing them luck, and were about to get on the train when an older African man appeared on the platform with a suitcase and a small duffle bag. His baggage made me realize that Lamin, Robert and Kibrom had none; they were travelling with nothing more than the clothes on their backs.

We approached the man and asked if he needed help. His appearance was rather shabby, he smelled like a homeless person, and he appeared to be in poor health. He sheepishly answered that he wanted to go to Stuttgart, but didn't have a ticket. The regional train we had planned to take was about to depart, so I told Giovanna and Carlos that I would take care of the man and let them leave. I asked him whether he had travel documents; he said that he did. He later explained that he was from Gambia and had an Italian residence permit, which allowed him to travel freely within the Schengen Area in conjunction with his passport. He had been kicked off the train because he was travelling without a ticket, not because of his travel documents.

After helping the man buy a ticket to Innsbruck from the Austrian ticket machine and suggesting taking a bus from there, since he didn't have enough money to go all the way by rail, I returned to the waiting room with him. He had a chat with Lamin in their local language – incomprehensible to me, but nonetheless giving every impression of the kind of small talk typical of unexpectedly meeting a fellow citizen far from home. He then explained that he arrived in Italy in 2011, ended up in Turin, but the social housing he lived in closed a few days earlier, so he became homeless. He spent three days on the streets of Turin (which, in mid-January, certainly isn't a situation that can last for long) and then decided to find shelter and perhaps a job in Stuttgart, where a friend lived.

I offered the man as many left-over sandwiches as he could carry, wished the three young men all the best, and headed home with a heavy heart. My first day volunteering brought me into contact with people who had experienced hardship and tragedy in ways I have never come close to. I felt a sense of admiration for the young men's resolve and sadness for the old man's poor fortune. They had all risked their lives to escape the disadvantage they were born into. They dared to create their own destinies. And despite it all, they weren't better off than before.

***

## The North Pole's unexpected visitors

I returned to the Brenner a few days later. My train ride offered a complete winter landscape all the way, as it snowed down to the lowest valleys overnight, and it was still snowing in the morning. The Brenner looked like the North Pole; a thick layer of snow covered everything, and gusts of wind periodically blew clouds of fine powder across the platforms.

I got off the train and immediately spotted a group of around 20 black and Middle Eastern-looking men crowding around a ticket machine, looking completely out of place. They were surely migrants heading north. Before approaching them, I looked for Hakim, an Iraqi who came to Italy as a refugee himself and who worked for Volontarius at the Brenner. Before I could find him, a man from the group approached me and asked, in fluent Italian, for help with the ticket machine, since it wasn't accepting cash. It was the same ticket machine that took Lamin and Robert's money a few days before, so I explained that it didn't work. I noticed that he was at least ten years older than the others in the group, who were in their early twenties at most, and unlike the others, he had a small suitcase. I asked him where he was from and whether he had travel documents; he answered saying that he was from Pakistan and assured me that his travel documents were in order.

Hakim finally appeared and hurried over to the group of Africans and Middle Easterners getting more and more frustrated with the ticket machine, and spoke to them in Arabic. Although I couldn't understand what he said, his words calmed them down somewhat, and everyone followed him into the waiting room after a brief talk. I tagged along, and asked Hakim what was going on while we walked down the platform. He told me that the group consisted of Somalis and Afghans who had been caught by Austrian police in Innsbruck and had been brought back to the Brenner just a little while before. They all wanted to go to Germany. I wanted to ask him about the Pakistani man, but we entered the waiting room before I had a chance, and Hakim spoke to them again in Arabic.

While Hakim was talking, the train to Munich rolled onto the platform, and upon sight of the train, the group became visibly agitated once more. Hakim and I stepped back outside to check whether other migrants had arrived on the train. We walked up the far end of the platform to where the Italian, Austrian and German police officers were joking about something, and didn't see anyone except for train personnel and a few incredibly resolute smokers braving the periodic clouds of snow being blown onto the platform. I asked Hakim about the Pakistani man; he suspected the man was a smuggler accompanying the Afghans – and likely making a lot of money off of them. We walked back to the waiting room, only to find it empty. The group had clearly taken advantage of the distracted police officers and clouds of snow obstructing the view down the platform to board the train.

After the train departed, we took refuge from the weather for a while inside the flat before heading back to the station to see if anyone had shown up. Indeed, when we returned, a group of around 15 Africans were roaming around the platforms. We approached them, and apparently recognizing them as Somalis due to their facial features, Hakim immediately spoke to them in Arabic. As with the previous group, we brought them to the waiting room, and promised to return with tea and cheese sandwiches, which we did a few minutes later.

Most of the Somalis seemed to be younger than those we had met earlier. In fact, a few looked like they weren't older than 14 or 15. They wolfed down the sandwiches we brought, and while passing out plastic cups filled with hot tea, I struck up a conversation with those who could speak English. They told me that they had crossed the Mediterranean only a few days earlier. One of the younger looking ones told me that he had seen a woman give birth on the boat he was on. They were rescued by the Italian Coast Guard, and shortly after arriving in Sicily, were told that they were free to go anywhere in Europe they wanted.

Their support for Bayern München football team and rumours of jobs in Germany led to their decision to head north. However, a tri-national police patrol found them on one of the Munich-bound international trains and made them get off in Bolzano. They were handed the usual document requesting them to appear at the local Questura to regularize their status, but they continued their journey with a regional train up to the Brenner.

After providing the group with food and drinks, Hakim and I went back to the flat to have lunch ourselves. When we returned to the station, the next international train was already at the platform, and the usual trio of police officers was chatting outside. We walked down to the waiting room to see if the Somalis were still there – it was empty. On our way back up the platform, we saw most of them inside the train's restaurant wagon. They were risking drawing attention to themselves, but another member of the group, who was further down the train, was spotted by the police officers first. The officers got on the train, and stepped off a few moments later with one of the younger looking ones. Now separated from the group, the boy stood alone on the platform, visibly frightened. When the Italian and German policemen stepped away from their Austrian colleague for a moment, who remained close to one of the train's doors, the boy begged him in English to let him get on the train. "Na!" barked the officer in Tyrolean dialect.

The international train heading south was delayed, causing the northbound train to stay at the platform for several minutes. Time slowed to a crawl as the officers chatted in front of the train while the boy looked at it longingly. Finally, the station's loudspeakers announced that the southbound train wouldn't arrive on the platform opposite the northbound one's like usual, but on another platform further away. The officers were waiting to take that train back to Trento in order to board another train going to Munich, and had to use an underpass to reach the other platform. As soon as they were out of sight, the Somali boy hurried back onboard. At last, the delayed train arrived, and the northbound train departed. All the Somalis were safely onboard. After a brief stop, the southbound train left as well, and silence returned to the now deserted station. Hakim and I returned to the flat.

The rest of the afternoon was quiet, so I decided to explore Brenner village. I had passed through countless times before, but had never stopped to actually see it. While walking around, I noticed that in many ways, it's very untypical of a village counting a few hundred residents. Its centrepiece is its disproportionately large train station, built in fascist-era architectural style which is visibly decaying after years of tough weather and a clear lack of maintenance. Parallel tracks for parked cargo trains occupy a large part of the narrow valley the village is located in, and on the other side of the tracks, a wooded mountain slope rises steeply towards barren summits a few hundred metres above. The Brenner motorway disappears in a tunnel inside the mountain for most of the length of the village, sparing it from noise and exhaust fumes.

The Brenner boasts a brand new factory outlet mall full of clothing stores that mainly attract Austrians looking for discounts, only a few steps from an old border guardhouse converted into a shop selling Lederhosen and Dirndl dresses. The village also has a few shops selling leather goods, alcohol and "speck" (a local type of bacon) at supposedly discount prices, a sausage stand, a train company dormitory and a small church. At the far end of the village, a massive police station and a slightly smaller Carabinieri (military police) station stand on a slight elevation. A discount supermarket marks the southern tip of the village.

After seeing the little there was to see, I headed back to the train station to check for migrants on the 18:00 train, but there were none. It was a Friday, and I had planned to spend the weekend in Innsbruck to visit friends there, so I boarded the next Austrian regional train half an hour later. During the short ride, I thought of how different my reality was from that of the refugees trying desperately to cross the border that day. They were confronted with a guarded wall and the constant threat of being discovered after crossing it;

while for me, there was practically no border at all. The only thing that changed for me was the mobile phone network.

At the same time I was comfortably approaching Innsbruck, a 22 year-old Eritrean risked his life to cross the border, as I read in the newspaper upon my return back home. He wanted to board the last international train of the day in Bolzano but was stopped by police on the platform. He walked away, hid somewhere, and when the train departed, he ran to the locomotive, grabbed a service railing and climbed onto a small footrest right above the rear bumper. A police officer saw him and shouted an order to get off, but the train gathered speed and he was out of sight. The policeman contacted the station manager, who contacted the train's driver, but by the time the message got through, the train had already passed through a long tunnel that starts just after Bolzano. Police found the young man still hanging on to the locomotive on the other side and took him to the local police station. After he was released, he vanished, surely to find another way to cross the border.

\*\*\*

## Switzerland's unwanted economist

I spent my third day at the Brenner with Hakim and another Volontarius employee, Amina, an Italian woman in her early 30s with Palestinian ancestry. When

I arrived in the morning, there were no migrants at the station, so the three of us spent some time chatting in the flat before we headed to the station to see if anyone was taken off the 12 o'clock train to Munich.

We arrived before the train did, but two African young men were standing in front of the same ticket machine that didn't work the week before. They had both arrived on a regional train a little while earlier and wanted to buy a ticket to Munich, but the machine apparently still hadn't been fixed. However, rather than take their money without printing a ticket, it simply wouldn't accept their banknotes. The other ticket machine at the station's entrance only accepted credit cards by design, and an Austrian rail company ticket machine on another platform wasn't accepting cash that day either. It almost seemed as if the ticket machines had been programmed to make life difficult for the number one group of travellers without bank accounts: refugees.

As it was impossible to buy a ticket with cash at the station, their only options were either to buy a ticket onboard, which would cost more, or riding without a ticket and risking to get kicked off and handed over to the police. The second option would of course be particularly risky due to their irregular migrant status. They decided to buy a ticket on board, but when the Munich train rolled in, the tri-national patrol kept an eye on the platform while chatting as usual. The two Africans decided to try getting on later trains, and ended up spending all day sitting next to the heating radiators in the waiting room, trying to keep warm and maintain their patience as the scene repeated itself each time the Munich-bound train arrived.

One of the Africans was an Eritrean in his late twenties, while the other was a Somali in his late teens/early twenties. Semere, the Eritrean, was a nervous wreck and constantly worried about getting caught by the police. Amadayo, the Somali, spoke only a few words in English and Arabic, so communicating with him was difficult. All I could understand was that he had been caught by Austrian police in Innsbruck the day before and was returned to the Brenner after spending the night at an Austrian transit centre for returnees. Semere, the Eritrean, spoke much better English, so I had a long conversation with him about his story.

Semere left Eritrea several years ago because he was imprisoned after being suspected of helping people cross the border between Eritrea and Ethiopia illegally. Semere denied doing anything of sorts, and told me he believes he was arrested simply because he lived close to the border and because his father is Ethiopian. He was released after six months, when his parents managed to pay bail, but he decided to leave the country before the trial – knowing that it wouldn't be fair. He moved to Ethiopia and studied at Addis Ababa University, where he graduated with a Bachelor's degree in Economics.

Semere showed me a photocopy of his diploma and his marks transcript, and it struck me that for him, his education was far more valuable than his citizenship. He didn't have a passport, he didn't have a residence permit, but he had a copy of his diploma with him. He was carrying what could be perhaps the most democratic travel document of all; one that isn't based solely on circumstances of birth, but on personal achievement as well.

After graduating, Semere found a well-paying job in Juba, South Sudan, where he stayed until civil war broke out in December 2013. He fled north to Khartoum, Republic of the Sudan, and only then decided to try reaching Europe. He spent 10 days crossing the Sahara desert into Libya on top of a truck loaded with other migrants, and told me that he nearly died in the middle of the trip. Dehydrated, he lost consciousness and fell off the truck onto the hot desert sand. Luckily, the driver stopped – which is rarely the case on such trips – and poured some energy drink into his mouth, which brought him back to his senses.

When the truck entered the first Libyan town after the border, all the migrants were arrested and imprisoned. Semere told me that hundreds of people were packed into a cell that was barely larger than the Brenner train station's waiting room, which is about 25 square metres. The guards were brutal, and treated the migrants like animals. He spent three weeks in prison, and then paid 1000 Libyan dinars (over 600 Euros) to be released. He continued his journey to Tripoli, and was arrested again. After a month in a prison similar to the first, he paid 1700 dinars (over 1000 Euros) to be released.

Semere's "welcome" to Libya made me wonder. In May 2013, the EU Integrated Border Management Assistance Mission in Libya (EUBAM Libya) was deployed with a two year mandate and an annual budget of 26 Million Euros. According to the mission's factsheet (January 2015 version):

*"EUBAM Libya supports the Libyan authorities in developing border management and security at the country's land, sea and air borders. As a civilian crisis management mission with a capacity-building mandate, EUBAM assists Libyan authorities at strategic and operational level. The work is carried out through advising, training and mentoring Libyan counterparts in strengthening the border services in accordance with international standards and best practices, and by advising the Libyan authorities on the development of a national Integrated Border Management (IBM) strategy."*

Semere entered Libya in early 2014, well into EUBAM Libya's mandate. I don't believe that the kind of treatment he received upon arrival in Libya is in accordance with international standards and best practices. I do believe that EUBAM needs to explain how border prisons that extort money from refugees can exist after almost a year of advising, training and mentoring.

In June of 2014, Semere crossed the Mediterranean and was rescued by Italy's Mare Nostrum operation after three days at sea. After arriving in Sicily, he headed north to Rome, and then to Milan. The number of homeless, unemployed migrants he saw roaming the streets in both cities spurred him on to look for better conditions further north. From Milan, he took a train to Switzerland and declared asylum there. He spent a month in a migrant reception centre (which he described as another stay in prison), and then moved into a migrant housing facility in Zurich.

Semere described Zurich as the most perfect city he had ever seen. It was clean, safe and prosperous – a world away from the torturous prisons of Libya. While waiting for the outcome of his asylum application, Semere attended German language courses and befriended one of the social workers at the facility. He thought he had finally made it, he thought he could finally settle down. Then, after five months, he was given a document stating the outcome of the asylum procedure: the Swiss authorities had determined that according to the Dublin Regulation, Italy was responsible for his asylum application and he would thus be returned to Italy within a few days.

Semere was put on a plane to Rome, and handed over to the Italian police, which gave him the option to either officially seek asylum in Italy or leave the country. Semere decided to leave and try getting asylum elsewhere, so he was given a document stating that he was obligated to leave Italy within a week, and would be fined between 10,000 – 20,000 Euros if he remained on Italian territory thereafter. Two days later, Semere made it to the Brenner on regional trains, hoping to be able to find a job and make use of his newly acquired language skills in Germany.

Late in the afternoon, shortly before I went home, four other African young men arrived on regional trains to the Brenner who also wanted to reach Germany. Two were from Nigeria; one was from Ghana and another from Gambia. The Nigerians had landed in Sicily two months before, while the other two had been in Italy slightly longer. All of them wanted to leave the lack of opportunity in Italy behind them. All of them wanted to go somewhere they could find a job. All of them wanted to take the 8 o'clock train to Munich.

Slightly over a week earlier, Kibrom, Lamin and Robert were in the exact same situation. I had exchanged e-mail addresses with Kibrom and friended Robert on Facebook. Kibrom wrote that he had made it to Munich and was in a refugee reception centre there. He was happy. Robert posted some pictures of himself posing in front of Munich's Allianz Arena – the home of Bayern München football team. They had made it. They had reached their Promised Land. But the big question remained: would they be allowed to stay, or would they be sent back to Italy like Semere was from Zurich?

\*\*\*

## Stranded Somalis

My next day at the Brenner was rather chaotic. When I arrived in the late morning, Amina was taking care of a group of eight young men from Iraq, Syria, Eritrea and Somalia who had spent the night in the waiting room. They had arrived on a regional train late the previous day, after the last train to Munich had already departed. All of them wanted to reach Germany except for one of the Syrians, who wanted to go to Finland.

The 12 o'clock EuroCity arrived shortly after I did, and with it, a visibly frustrated Gambian woman accompanied by her eight or nine year-old daughter. The police had kicked them off the train, but she didn't understand why. I asked her whether she had valid travel documents, and she said that she did, and showed me her Italian identification card stating that she was a resident of a town in northern Italy. Unlike usual, the police officers didn't stand on the platform after getting off, so lacking the possibility of clarification and lacking the presence of obstacles, she decided to get back on the train with her daughter and large suitcase. The lack of police also created an opportunity for the group of young men, who also got on the train undetected. Yet another group of refugees were on their way north.

A little while later, three Africans appeared on the far end of one of the platforms: two young men who looked barely over 18, and a girl who later told me she was 15. The girl spoke English best, and told me that they were all from Somalia and had been caught by police in Innsbruck, then brought to the police station here, in this little village in the middle of nowhere, of which she didn't know the name, or whether it was in Italy or Austria. All she knew was that her sister was still inside the police station with some other Somalis they were travelling with, and was worried about her.

The three of them wanted to stay on the frigid platform outside to keep a look out for the others still with the police, but Amina and I convinced them to wait in the warmth of the station's self-service café: a barren room with nothing but a few vending machines and big windows facing the direction they expected their friends to come from. Sure enough, one by one, they showed up; in total they were 5 young men with bad teeth and 5 girls wearing headscarves, including the 15 year-olds' big sister, aged 19.

All of them had been given the usual document summoning them to Bolzano's police station to regularize their status, but none of them knew what it meant. While trying to explain the document to them, which was difficult due to their very limited English, I realized that they didn't even know what asylum meant. All they knew was that they wanted to leave Italy to reach brothers, sisters and friends in Norway, Sweden and Germany. No one had made it clear to them since their arrival in Sicily two weeks earlier that they were not allowed to leave Italy, and would need to claim asylum in order to stay anywhere in Europe, for that matter.

Nevertheless, the group decided to try to proceed to Munich, and spent the rest of the afternoon trying to board the international trains heading north unsuccessfully. A friendly-looking German policewoman who stayed onboard one of the trains to head home after her shift stopped one of the Somalis from getting onboard in a much different way than the Austrian officer I had seen the week before. With a smile, in English, she said, "not on this train"...

As time passed, the group became more and more restless. The boys would periodically argue with each other, in what appeared to be mutual accusations of messing up their chances of getting on the trains. When they weren't arguing, they were talking on their mobile phones in agitated voices. The girls started crying. They were only an hour and a half away from the German border, but that border was quickly becoming a mirage, impossible to reach, like one of the many they must have seen in the Sahara desert.

After the 6 o'clock EuroCity came and left without them, they decided to give up and go to Bolzano. I offered to accompany them, since I was planning on taking the next regional train home and would pass through Bolzano anyway. However, shortly before the train was scheduled to leave, the group split up and was scattered all over the station – the girls in tears, the boys exasperated. I had to leave, but Amina stayed with them and offered to accompany them to Bolzano with the next train an hour later.

I texted Amina later in the evening to ask how things went. They changed their minds about going to Bolzano and decided to stay at the Brenner. The next morning, she texted me saying that some of them ended up in Bressanone; the others disappeared.

\*\*\*

## Desperate souls in a desperate country

Every day at the Brenner was different. Some days brought big groups of exasperated refugees, while others brought a handful of calm and comfortable ones. Some were able to get on trains heading north without any problems, others had much more difficulty penetrating the Inner Wall. It seemed to be more a question of luck than anything else.

The beginning of my next week at the Brenner brought the second type of migrants. The day started slowly; no one showed up until the mid-afternoon, when two young men from Morocco arrived on a regional train from the south and two young men from Somalia were released from the Brenner police station. The Moroccans wanted to reach family members in the Netherlands; they had landed in Sicily only six days earlier. The Somalis had been in Italy for a few months, realized that there was nothing there for them, and decided to head north. Austrian police caught them in Innsbruck and returned them to the Brenner, but they were eager to continue their journey, unfazed by the temporary set-back.

When the four o'clock Munich-bound train arrived, the Somalis made a risky, but successful move and boarded the train while the tri-national patrol was walking up the platform away from them. The Moroccans decided that it was too risky. They stayed in the waiting room to try again on the next train, and planned to lock themselves in the toilets all the way to Munich.

The two of them only spoke Arabic, but I managed to learn a little bit about them through Hakim, who interpreted as I asked them a few questions. The young men were childhood friends who came from poor families. They quit school early in order to work, but couldn't earn enough in Morocco to support their ageing parents and younger siblings. Two years ago, they left home to find better-paid work elsewhere, which they did as construction workers in Libya.

Unlike Kibrom and Semere, they were treated reasonably well in Libya. Perhaps their lighter skin colour and common language helped them stand out less; perhaps there exists some sort of North African solidarity that doesn't extend to dark-skinned peoples on the other side of the Sahara. Nevertheless, Libya's increasing political instability and internal armed conflict since the fall of the Gaddafi regime made a continued stay too dangerous. The two of them never intended to come to Europe, but lacking other options, decided to cross the Mediterranean Sea to Italy.

One thing that one of the two said touched me. He said that he risked his life and is willing to live far away from home not for himself, not to improve his own life, but to send money back to his parents. He told me that without the money he sent them from Libya, they would be homeless. He needed to find another job quickly, before their meagre reserves dried up. I admired his altruism, but given his Arabic-only language skills, feared that he wouldn't be able to find a job in the Netherlands quickly enough to prevent his parents from living on the streets.

Shortly before the 6 o'clock train arrived, a 20-something year old from Ghana arrived on a regional train. He told me that he had been in Italy for three years, had a residence permit, but led a miserable life of homelessness and unemployment first in southern Italy and then in Rome. He was fed up. He wanted to start a new life in Austria, where he hoped things would be better.

He had no money and hadn't eaten in two days, so I gave him the last three sandwiches we had along with some tea. While he wolfed down the sandwiches, I explained that due to his Italian residence permit, he was almost certainly not going to be allowed to stay in Austria. I told him that the Austrian police would return him, but he said that he wanted to try anyway. He simply didn't want to stay in Italy, no matter what.

When the train arrived, something unexpected happened. Two Italian police officers saw me and Hakim talking to the Ghanaian in the waiting room, entered it, and without even asking him where he was going, told him in plain English that he should take the next train, since there would be no police on it. With a reassuring smile, they left.

To northern European countries, Italy's disregard of the Dublin Regulation and dishonest implementation of bilateral agreements seems outrageous. However, can one really blame the Italians? They have demonstrated genuine humanitarian good-will by conducting the large-scale Mare Nostrum search and rescue operation largely at their own cost. Yet Italy has been mostly left alone by its European partners to deal with a massive influx of refugees at a time when its economy is fragile at best. At the same time, Italy has been hosting an increasing number of migrants who would rather live elsewhere.

Isn't it rather outrageous to force migrants with family and friends in northern Europe, migrants who speak a northern European language, migrants who have professional skills needed in northern Europe, to stay trapped in Italy to face a life on the streets? Isn't it outrageous to turn a blind eye to the plight of people fleeing war and misery not unlike northern Europeans themselves did only 70 years ago? Isn't it outrageous to preach European solidarity and practice national insulation?

# Part 2: Stories from Europe's Purgatory

## African predicaments and European failures

Over the course of several weeks at the Brenner, I met many more migrants heading north. They had different backgrounds, came from different countries and had different stories about how they ended up reaching the Inner Wall. Some reached it a few days after crossing the Mediterranean Sea, while some spent years in Italy before heading north. All of them, with a few exceptions, were trying to reach the better future they had left home for, but which Italy couldn't provide. All of them were stuck in an unexpected limbo – some for just a little while, others for longer – stranded in a place located between their hopes for the future and the hard realities of their pasts. Some of my more memorable encounters are described in this chapter.

Franklin, a man in his early 30s from Benin City, Nigeria, was one of the many who decided to leave Italy after finding that it simply couldn't be the final destination he had risked his life to reach. Franklin left Benin City in 2008. The once-proud capital of the powerful Kingdom of Benin was burned down by the British in 1897 and subsequently incorporated into British Nigeria. Since Nigeria's independence in 1960, the city has gained a reputation as the capital of Nigeria's sex trade. Poverty and lacking education have made local girls prime targets for human trafficking rings that smuggle them to Europe to work as prostitutes. That same poverty and lacking education prompted Franklin to head to Europe on his own accord, in order to find work and perhaps a better education.

Franklin headed north to Agadez, Niger, a city on the southern edge of the Sahara Desert that has become a sort of base camp for West African migrants attempting to cross the desert into Libya. On his way to Agadez, he was robbed by police and bandits alike, but managed to hide some of his money well enough to pay his way north. From Agadez, he continued his trip on top of a truck loaded with other migrants, which slowly made its way northeast into the desert toward Libya. In Dirkou, the next town along the route, he unexpectedly met his brother, who had left Nigeria a month earlier. His brother had been robbed of all of his belongings, and was stuck in this dangerous outpost in the middle of the desert as a result. Franklin still had enough money to pay smugglers for his brother's trip as well, so they left Dirkou together and entered Libya a few days later.

The two of them needed more money to pay for their Mediterranean crossing, so they worked in a bakery in Libya before heading to a beach near Tripoli that smugglers used to board them and hundreds of others onto a boat heading to Italy. After several miserable days at sea, the brothers were found by the Italian Coast Guard and taken to Lampedusa, where they spent two weeks in the island's initial reception centre. From there, they were flown to Gorizia, a town in northeast Italy close to the Slovenian border, and their asylum applications were processed there. Both of them were rejected. They appealed the decision with the help of a lawyer in Brescia, a city in north central Italy, and decided to move there together.

Their appeal was not successful, but instead of returning to Nigeria, they stayed in Italy illegally. They spent the next six years begging on the streets of Brescia to survive. They learned almost no Italian in this period; all the language schools they tried to enrol in wanted to see documents before signing them up. Their chances of finding work without documents and without language skills stayed as low as when they first arrived. They were hardly better off than they were in Nigeria, but returning home empty handed would bring shame upon themselves and their family.

Finally, Franklin's brother decided to try his luck in Germany with a Nigerian girl he fell in love with in Brescia. Four months later, Franklin decided to follow suit. He bought a ticket for the international train from Verona to Munich, and was on his way north when the tri-national police patrol boarded the train in Trento, spotted the suspicious black man and asked him for his documents. He could only offer the documents that he had certainly used to fend off police checks before: the confirmation of his original asylum application from 2008, along with some paperwork from his lawyer in Brescia which gave the impression that he was still awaiting a final asylum decision. What helped him avoid deportation in Italy was of no use to cross the border into Austria, however. The police kicked him off the train in Bolzano.

Franklin continued his journey on a regional train to the Brenner. He arrived on a clear and crisp evening with a duffle bag and a small suitcase, ready to catch one of the international trains he had been kicked off of. Ready to reunite with his brother in Munich. Ready to find a reason for his risky journey to Europe.

Abubacar, a young man from Guinea-Bissau I met a few days later, was becoming a desperate beggar like Franklin when he got unexpected help from a white man. Abubacar told me his story in a level of English that was better than that of most migrants I met at the Brenner, despite the fact that he had never gone to school. He learned it himself out of necessity. He had a tender face with a gentle expression, but a large scar on his forehead and the leather-like skin on his hands suggested a rough past.

Guinea-Bissau is a former Portuguese colony that gained independence in 1974. The small West African country on the Atlantic Ocean is one of the poorest nations on earth, with a per capita Gross National Income (GNI) of USD 590 in 2013, according to the World Bank.[1] In situations of extreme poverty, conflict over scarce resources is inevitable, and religious

---

[1] For more economic information on Guinea-Bissau, see:
http://data.worldbank.org/country/guinea-bissau

differences can easily fuel accusations of injustice. Abubacar became a victim of such circumstances. He belonged to the country's Muslim majority, but worked for a Christian. Some fellow Muslims called him a traitor and pressured him to stop working for the Christian man. Abubacar refused, and got his scar as a result.

Frightened by the incident, and unable to find alternative work at home, he decided to leave his country in 2010, when he was 19 years old. Abubacar spent the next four years roaming around West Africa, looking for and collecting scrap metal that he could sell for some money. At one point, he decided to try to find a better life in Europe. He made his way to Libya, where he worked as a day labourer laying brinks. Once he earned (and hid) enough money to pay smugglers, he crossed the Mediterranean and arrived in Sicily in February of 2014.

Immediately after landing in Sicily, he was flown to a reception centre in Cagliari, on the island of Sardinia, where his asylum application was processed and rejected. He appealed the decision with the help of a local NGO, and started begging on the streets of Cagliari. Abubacar described the city as a hopeless place where African migrants like him slowly went mad. Local residents gave them the cold shoulder, and the geographical isolation of the island essentially trapped them there. The ferry to mainland Italy was too expensive for an escape.

One day, while begging, a white man handed him 50 Euros – enough to buy a ferry ticket to Rome. Abubacar left immediately. He decided to join his older brother, who had managed to reach Germany a few months earlier. Abubacar made it without problems, and requested asylum in Germany, despite his still-open appeal in Cagliari. The German authorities took him to a reception centre in a town in north-central Germany. He was given an asylum-seeker identification card that required him to stay in the federal state of Saxony-Anhalt, where the town is located. Abubacar marvelled at his new home. He called Germany his favourite country. The conditions were far better than in Cagliari; he was being taken care of. He wanted to stay, despite the incredibly cold weather.

A few months later, his younger brother arrived in Sicily. He had made it across the Mediterranean Sea alive, but wasn't in good health. The strains of the trip had worn him down, and he seemed confused. Abubacar hadn't seen his brother in years and was worried, so he decided to visit him, simply leaving his German identification card behind. He didn't realize that by doing so, he risked being fined, and that trying to return to Germany without documents had become much more difficult since he had first made the trip.

Abubacar met his brother in Sicily, but his brother wasn't himself. He was homeless and unemployed; Abubacar wanted to bring him to Germany, but his brother refused. He refused to go anywhere. He had made it to Europe – in his mind, his trip was over. The lack of food and shelter didn't make any difference to him. He had gone mad. Abubacar returned alone. On board the international train between Trento and Verona, police found him and kicked him off in Bolzano. He was asked his name, birth date and nationality, and they were entered in a document inviting him to the Questura of Bolzano the next day to regularize his status in Italy. It was the same document that all the other undocumented migrants who got kicked off of the trains received, despite the fact that he already had an asylum procedure awaiting a final decision in Cagliari, and another open application in Germany. No one bothered to check.

Abubacar continued his journey on a regional train to the Brenner. There, he managed to get onboard the next international train to Munich, but one of the passengers alerted the police standing outside on the platform that he had got on the train and locked himself in one of the toilets. He was kicked off without further ado. The next train arrived two hours later, and Abubacar did the same thing, this time successfully.

Abubacar's story is a story of the complete failure of Europe's asylum system, both in terms of its implementation as well as its human cost. Abubacar was denied the international protection he should have received in Italy, he was able to cross borders that he shouldn't have been able to cross, and he started a second asylum procedure that he shouldn't have been able to start. But who could blame him for leaving the isolated hopelessness of Sardinia, where he could only await the distant outcome of an appeal unlikely to be successful? Who could blame him for leaving Saxony-Anhalt to see his ailing brother in Sicily after years of separation?

The story of a 20 year-old Eritrean I met the same day as Abubacar is perhaps an even better example of how clearly European asylum laws are out of tune with the realities that refugees face. The young man arrived in Italy in 2013, and was taken to Turin, where he was required to start his asylum procedure. However, his mother and uncle were in Sweden, so he didn't show up to the initial asylum interview in Turin. Instead, he travelled all the way to Sweden to reach his family members. He requested asylum there, but because he was over 18, he wasn't allowed to stay with his mother. He was sent back to Italy in accordance with the Dublin Regulation. Upon his arrival back in Italy, he was informed that he had been denied asylum because he had missed the interview in Turin, and thus needed to leave the country. With no options left, he decided to try going back to Sweden, but was kicked off the international train at the Brenner on his way north.

The young Eritrean was kicked off the train along with a Syrian man who said he had been slapped by police in Sicily because he didn't understand what they told him, two Nigerians who angrily complained about terrible conditions in a refugee housing facility in Rome, and a man from Ghana who had spent years trying unsuccessfully to get a residence permit from the

Questura in Naples. All of them were fed up with Italy. Italy was fed up with them. Their only hope was to head north, but the Inner Wall stood firmly in their way.

\*\*\*

## Opportunists, smugglers and undocumented tourists

To be fair, not everyone I saw passing through the Brenner without proper travel documents was in a dire situation. Among the countless desperate souls seeking an existential minimum in northern Europe, there were also opportunists and people who had no intention of leaving Italy for good. However, they represented a small minority of those who attempted to cross the border illegally.

One of the opportunists I encountered was a young man from India who had an expired Italian residence permit. He said that he had come back from Germany, where he worked, to renew it, but he was already on his way out of Italy again. Clearly, he couldn't spend too much time away from his undeclared job in Germany, so he didn't wait for the new card to arrive before heading back. Someone would certainly mail it to him when it was ready, and once he had it, any German police officer who checked his documents would think he was only a tourist.

A group of men with a peculiar story I met several days later claimed to be tourists, but I had my doubts. A short, rotund man with a Turkish accent accompanied by three tall, older Middle Eastern-looking men with solemn expressions on their faces asked me for help using the ticket machine to buy tickets to Innsbruck. They had arrived on a regional train from Verona. I asked him where he and his friends were from and where they were heading. He said that they were all from Denmark, and cheerfully explained that they were going back home after visiting friends in Italy. I asked him why they would take the train for such a long trip, and he answered briefly that their friends had recommended against driving or flying, due to winter weather. Even so, I wondered, why would they make the trip on regional trains and without buying tickets in advance? Was the supposedly Danish man with a Turkish accent perhaps in the company of wealthy Syrian refugees able to pay a smuggler to escort them to Sweden, which guarantees asylum to Syrians who manage to get there? Had they travelled a few weeks later, the questions in my head would have probably been asked by Austrian police officers, who started patrolling regional trains between the Brenner and Innsbruck after the loophole became evident.

A very friendly young man I met named Lumusi, from Togo, really did want to be nothing more than a tourist in Germany. I found him at the Brenner one morning after he had been returned from Innsbruck by the Austrian police. He was awaiting the result of an appeal against his negative asylum decision in Italy but had a job as a bricklayer in a small town in the central Apennines, which kept him quite happy to stay where he was. He had been in Italy for one and a half years, but had not yet visited his brother in Munich and sister in Koblenz, who both had residence permits and already visited him in Italy twice. Now it was Lumusi's turn to see them and the Teutonic lands they kept telling him about.

Lumusi wasn't lucky. His second attempt at crossing the border on the two o'clock train failed as well, since Austrian police conducting a patrol from the Brenner to Innsbruck caught him once again. They were the very same officers that caught him the first time. He was brought back to the Brenner on a police van in time for a third attempt on the six o'clock train. He had spent over 300 Euros on train tickets to reach his brother and sister, and had no money to spare, so giving up was out of the question for him.

Despite the constant set-backs, he was upbeat and talkative, so I asked Lumusi why he left his country. It was because of a girl, and the story was quite tragic. In Togo, he fell in love with the daughter of an Army officer and wanted to marry her. Her father didn't approve of the marriage, so the girl decided to run away from home. Since her father was a well-connected man, she knew that she would be found and taken back home by force if she stayed in Togo, so she paid fishermen to bring her to Gabon by boat – an over

1,000 km trip across the Gulf of Guinea. Perhaps due to a lack of preparation, sickness, or simply the strains of such a long trip by boat, she died shortly after arriving in Gabon.

Upon hearing the news of his daughter's death, the girl's father accused Lumusi of orchestrating the escape (which he vehemently denied) and killing his daughter. Lumusi was arrested. His parents freed him on bail, but he knew that the trial wouldn't be fair so he left the country immediately. His brother and sister had already left for Europe, so with few other options, he decided to follow suit. Four months later, after crossing Benin, Niger and Libya, he made it to Sicily.

Another undocumented – or in his case underdocumented – tourist I met was a young man from Ghana who wanted to visit his aunt in Munich. He lived in Siena and had a residence permit, but no passport, which he would have needed to carry along with his residence permit card in order to visit other Schengen countries. He had lost his passport in the chaos of Libya, but couldn't afford the 200+ Euro fee to get a new one from the Ghanaian embassy. Would it be so difficult for European countries to agree to mutually recognize residence permit cards as travel documents the same way they already recognize identification cards for EU citizens?

\*\*\*

# Fleeing Boko Haram, Libyan prisons and Sicilian reception centres

If bureaucratic roadblocks didn't stop black market workers, smugglers and penniless travellers, they certainly didn't stop desperate refugees fleeing poor conditions in Sicily. Two friends from Nigeria, whom I met at the Brenner one morning after they had spent the night in the waiting room, were a perfect example. They had been kicked off the 8 o'clock train the evening before, proving that even the last train of the day wasn't always safe to take.

The two young men were Christians from southern Nigeria who had found jobs in Kano, northern Nigeria, before they left their country. Joseph worked in a pharmacy, while Godwin was a plumber. With an income and friends in Kano, they had no intention of leaving until Boko Haram, a fundamentalist terrorist organization seeking to create an Islamic state in Muslim-dominated northern Nigeria, made life in Kano too dangerous for them to stay. In late 2011, Boko Haram began targeting southern Nigerians living in the north through a campaign of violence which included several church bombings. In early January of 2012, Boko Haram set a three day ultimatum for southern Nigerians to leave the north, after which they started a series of bombings and shootings that culminated in a day of terror in Kano on January 20.[2]

Frightened by the attacks, Joseph and Godwin decided to leave Kano. Partly due to a military blockade preventing them to head south easily and partly because of hopes of better employment opportunities abroad, they decided to head north to Libya via Niger. They crossed the desert on a pick-up truck loaded with 35 migrants, but what they found in Libya wasn't much better than what they had left behind: violence, hostility towards Christians, and the constant threat of getting robbed. They considered going back to Nigeria, but decided against crossing the desert a second time after hearing the story of a friend who tried to return. Somewhere in the desert on his way back from Libya, he fell off the truck he was riding, but the truck didn't stop. He wandered around the desert alone for days before he was rescued by a truck heading the opposite direction, which brought him back to Libya.

Since staying in Libya was pointless and returning home was too dangerous, Joseph and Godwin decided to proceed to Europe. They were extremely lucky to find a compassionate Libyan who helped them stay safe and even paid for their trip across the Mediterranean. They were put on a small inflatable raft with 140-odd other migrants, one of whom had been given a crash

---

[2] The Boko Haram attacks are described in detail in a Human Rights Watch report available at:
http://www.hrw.org/news/2012/01/23/nigeria-boko-haram-widens-terror-campaign

course on how to steer it by the smugglers who organized the trip. The "captain" was also given and shown how to use a satellite phone, which would be used to call for help once the raft got close enough to Italy.

After three days at sea, they were rescued by the Italian Coast Guard and brought to Porto Empedocle, Sicily. Upon their arrival, they were taken to a reception centre further inland. According to Joseph and Godwin, the conditions in the reception centre – an agglomeration of poorly maintained containers – were terrible. The amenities were severely lacking and the reception centre's workers treated migrants disrespectfully. Rumours of better conditions in Germany prompted Joseph and Godwin to leave the centre after only a month, so they found themselves at the Brenner a few days later.

Kuto, a young man from Gambia I met who had been caught in Innsbruck and brought back to the Brenner the next day, couldn't stand the Sicilian reception centre he was in for more than three weeks. He had arrived in Sicily after spending three years in a Libyan prison; he was arrested during his first attempt at crossing the Mediterranean Sea. He and hundreds of other migrants were on a beach near Tripoli, ready to board a smuggler's boat, when Libyan police stormed the beach. A policeman slammed the back of his rifle into Kuto's face, causing him to almost completely lose eyesight on one of his eyes. Kuto was then brought to an overcrowded prison and stayed there until he managed to talk a guard into accepting a 1000 dollar bribe to let him go, which was transferred to him by family members and friends back home.

After hearing what he had gone through to get to Italy, I was convinced: if someone who endured three years of prison in Libya decided to leave an Italian reception centre after only three weeks, the conditions there must really be bad. But not everyone who arrived in Sicily actually ended up in a reception centre, as I learned from two young Eritreans who were at the Brenner only 5 days after arriving on Lampedusa.

The two young men spent only a few days on Lampedusa after they were rescued on the rough seas of mid-winter, and were then flown to an airport near Brescia in northern Italy along with a planeload of other migrants. Upon their arrival, around half of the migrants on the plane were taken to a police station to be fingerprinted and then transferred to a reception centre. The others were put on a bus, driven to a parking lot on the outskirts of Brescia, and told to get out. They were on their own. One of the Eritreans had a friend in Frankfurt, so he and his friend headed north to reach him.

While the experience these two Eritreans described to me went plainly against Italy's obligations under international and EU law, given the circumstances in Italy, it was possibly the most humane treatment they could get. They were rescued, for which they were both deeply thankful, and instead of being forced into likely miserable conditions in an overcrowded reception centre and unemployment beyond, they were set free. With no fingerprints in the EURODAC database and a geographical head start due to their location in northern Italy, they were free to find a better life in places where a better life was still possible.

*** 

## Italy's migrant dilemma

According to the 1951 Convention Relating to the Status of Refugees, which is the international legal basis for asylum, a refugee is a person who:

*"owing to well-founded fear of being persecuted for reasons of race, religion, nationality, membership of a particular social group or political opinion, is outside the country of his nationality and is unable or, owing to such fear, is unwilling to avail himself of the protection of that country; or who, not having a nationality and being outside the country of his former habitual residence as a result of such events, is unable or, owing to such fear, is unwilling to return to it."* [3]

All European Union member states have signed and ratified the Convention, as well as the EU Charter of Fundamental Rights, which states in Article 18 that:

---

[3] Article 1 A.(2) Convention Relating to the Status of Refugees

*"The right to asylum shall be guaranteed with due respect for the rules of the Geneva Convention of 28 July 1951 and the Protocol of 31 January 1967 relating to the status of refugees and in accordance with the Treaty on European Union and the Treaty on the Functioning of the European Union".[4]*

In order to turn the generously-worded theory of asylum law into practice, EU member states have implemented the so-called Qualification Directive, which provides a more detailed definition of who qualifies for asylum. Nevertheless, it leaves plenty of room for interpretation, and a narrow interpretation of the directive is often the reason for a rejected asylum application. However, many migrants who don't receive asylum are granted so-called subsidiary protection instead. According to Article 15 of the Qualification Directive, subsidiary protection can be granted if an applicant faces serious harm consisting of the death penalty, execution, torture or inhuman or degrading treatment or punishment in the country of origin, or serious and individual threat to a civilian's life or person by reason of indiscriminate violence in situations of international or internal armed conflict.[5]

Furthermore, according to Italian law, a foreigner cannot be denied a residence permit if there are serious reasons of a humanitarian nature for the individual to stay,[6] so migrants who don't qualify for asylum or

---

[4] Article 18 EU Charter of Fundamental Rights
[5] Article 15 EU Qualification Directive
[6] Art. 5 (6) Dlgs 286/98

subsidiary protection can and often do receive a so-called "residence permit for humanitarian reasons". The dilemma this has caused for Italy as the number of migrants has steadily increased in recent years was illustrated perfectly by a group of Tunisians and a group of Ethiopians who found themselves at the Brenner at the same time one day. The Tunisians had arrived in Italy four years before the Ethiopians, and the circumstances of the Tunisians' arrival more or less directly caused the conditions faced by the Ethiopians.

The Tunisians left their country in the turmoil of the 2011 Tunisian Revolution, which overthrew long-time dictator Zine El Abidine Ben Ali and inspired the Arab Spring. While the young men weren't specifically targeted, the overall security situation and unemployment prompted them to leave. One of them told me that he got into trouble with the police after he tried to sell toys at a market without a licence. He couldn't afford the licence, and he couldn't afford to bribe the police, so the police confiscated all of his toys, and threw them away along with his livelihood. When the group reached Italy, they applied for asylum but were only granted a residence permit for humanitarian reasons. They learned how to speak Italian half-way fluently and looked for work, but couldn't find any. After four years, they decided to leave Italy's hopeless lack of opportunity behind and apply for asylum again in Germany.

The Ethiopians were at the Brenner only a week after crossing the Mediterranean Sea. They belonged to the Oromo ethnic group, which has faced relentless discrimination and persecution by the Ethiopian government for many years.[7] One of the young men in the group explained that he was threatened soon after entering university – he had drawn attention to himself simply because of his high marks. Another young man's parents' house was expropriated for no apparent reason. These people fit the classic definition of refugee, and would have almost certainly been granted asylum if they could have stated their case, but weren't even given the chance. They disembarked an Italian Coast Guard ship on a rainy day in Sicily, and roamed around freely until they found an abandoned building to take shelter in. When the rain stopped, they headed north, since the wife of one of them had made it to Germany shortly before.

The Tunisians' residence permits spared them from deportation and gave them the chance to look for a job, but they and many others like them came during Italy's economic crisis, when Italians themselves struggled to find work. As the crisis persisted and more migrants arrived, an ever-increasing number of unemployed residence permit holders were trapped in Italy, unable to live elsewhere legally because they were registered in Italy. Apparently, at some point, the Italian government realized that registering migrants wasn't doing anyone a favour, so at least a portion of new arrivals were simply

---

[7] More information available in an Amnesty International report: https://www.amnesty.org/en/documents/AFR25/006/2014/en/

not registered from then on. The group of Ethiopians, and the two Eritreans I had spoken to before, were among them.

It would be unfair to label the Tunisians as plain and simple economic migrants, the Ethiopians as "real refugees", and blame the situation on an influx of economic migrants when the reality is much more complex and the problems mainly structural. While the Tunisians may not have experienced the kind of ethnic persecution that the Ethiopians did, they chose to leave at a time when Tunisia could have easily descended into chaos like Egypt did, or civil war as in Syria, at any moment. Going back now would mean going back to a growing Islamic State presence at home and in Libya next door. One of the Tunisians even suggested that he would commit suicide if he couldn't stay in Germany, since he didn't want to be homeless in Italy or risk getting beheaded back in Tunisia.

When that day's six o'clock train arrived, and the tri-national patrol got off, an Italian officer peered into the waiting room without opening the glass doors, and saw the group of Tunisians, the Ethiopians, as well as three Eritrean teenagers and a 20 year-old from Gambia inside. The officer turned to Hakim, who was standing outside nearby, and said that he felt sorry for them, but also wondered whether any of them were infiltrated Islamic State terrorists. Hakim assured him none of them were, and the officer said they could get on the next train, which wouldn't be checked.

## Local reactions: solidarity, protest and deception

As Northern Europe hid behind the Inner Wall and Italy was left alone with its dilemma, the injustice of it all was expressed by increasingly desperate actions by migrants, and displays of solidarity by train passengers and civil society. In the space of less than one week in February, local newspapers reported about two separate instances in which migrants attempted to reach Munich on foot – walking along the railway line. An Ethiopian was seen walking inside a tunnel by a startled cargo train driver, who alerted the police. A few days later, four migrants from Sudan were caught doing the same thing. Railway traffic was halted for the duration of their retrieval, and all of them were charged with the offense of interrupting a public service.

A young man from Gambia who was kicked off a train at the Brenner one afternoon garnered the sympathy of an Italian old man who watched from the train's open doorway as police officers refused to let the Gambian back onboard. I watched as the young man begged the officers to let him reach his brother in Munich, and the old man – thinking that the Gambian was only being blocked because he didn't have a ticket – offered to pay for the young man's trip. The police officers gave the old man an unmistakable look of disapproval, and stood firm until the train left.

On March 1, 2015, roughly 200 people came to the Brenner to demonstrate against the tri-lateral police patrols, Austria's returns and the Dublin Regulation in general. It was the largest demonstration ever to take place in the small village, bringing together a wide range of civil society groups from Italy, Austria and Germany. The variety of groups was reflected in the plethora of messages on display: flags and banners stating "Refugees Welcome" and "No Person is Illegal", but also proclaiming "Capitalism is good...nowhere! Borders are shit...everywhere!" or "No law, no order, destroy the border", or even "Fire and Flames to the Deportation Authorities".

I am not a fan of the radical political left, even less so of anarchists, and often find that such groups inadvertently sabotage some good intentions that their ideologies contain. Extreme positions and provocative statements like some of those on display at the Brenner only serve to link migration with communism and anarchism, making refugees as repulsive as those ideologies are to the average citizen. Toning down the rhetoric even just a little bit would avoid alienating people that would otherwise have an open ear for the pro-immigrant cause. One of the signs that were held up during the Brenner demonstration was a perfect example of such moderation: "Refugees Welcome – Freedom for people, not just goods".

Those on the political left weren't the only ones protesting the situation caused by the police patrols and Austria's returns. A few days before the large demonstration, a small delegation of Italy's right-wing, anti-immigrant Northern League gathered at Bolzano's train station to accuse the provincial government of jeopardizing Bolzano's security by supporting Mare Nostrum, releasing prisoners and decriminalizing irregular immigration. As wild as the accusations were, they probably resonated better with local concerns about the recent arrivals than signs at the Brenner demanding "No law, no order, destroy the border".

While the political far-left and far-right wanted to draw attention to the issue in their own ways, the governing centre-right wanted to sweep it under the rug. When journalists from Rai Tre, one of Italy's large national TV channels, came to Bolzano to conduct interviews and gather film footage at the train station for a news report about the situation, no migrants were to be seen. An order from above requested the police to kick migrants off the international trains in Bressanone instead of Bolzano while the Rai Tre camera crew was at the station. It was a shameful way to hide a shameful situation, and the police union itself criticized the order in a local newspaper article two days later.

\*\*\*

# The Italian migrant who changed his mind about migrants

Faced with the current wave of migrants coming from Africa and the Middle East, Europeans often forget that their own ancestors emigrated en masse not too long ago. The suspicions and stereotypes attached to the current wave of newcomers sound hollow when compared to Europeans' own record abroad. An encounter I had with an Italian man at the Brenner was a case in point.

The man was in his late 50s, was half a head shorter than me and had a trimmed gray moustache giving him a down-to-earth, fatherly appearance. He introduced himself in a thick southern Italian accent: Salvio, from Calabria, and he was stranded at the Brenner on his way north to his sister in Cologne. He told me that he had spent the night in the waiting room because he had no money – he had been robbed at the train station in Verona while taking a nap between trains. He still had his bank card, but no money on his account, so he asked his sister to transfer enough to continue his trip, and was waiting for the money to become available for withdrawal.

Salvio was a very talkative man, and explained that he left Calabria when his financial reserves ran dry – he couldn't find a job at home, he still wasn't old enough to receive a pension, and decided to join his sister in Germany to look for a job there. He planned to take regional trains all the way to save money, and even told me about a discount flat-rate ticket he knew would be available in Bavaria, which he intended to buy immediately after crossing the border. The theft of his meagre reserves in Verona clearly frustrated him very much, and Salvio blamed it on foreigners – "all criminals", he said. Salvio thought it was probably Albanians who stole his money, since he knew they were especially bad troublemakers.

This statement hit a nerve in me, and I immediately countered with a speech about how one cannot generalize migrants like that. I reminded him that countless members of his parents' and grandparents' generation immigrated to the United States and brought southern Italy's mafia with them. If he were American, I asked, wouldn't he say that all Italians are criminals? Realizing the mistaken logic of his rant against Albanians, he revised his statement somewhat – not all of them are criminals, but many are. Why else would they come to Italy? And all of the Africans flooding into Lampedusa; what do they want if everyone knows there are no jobs in Italy? Surely they don't even want to work!

The answer to his questions and assumptions materialized in the form of a young Eritrean girl and an even younger boy who arrived at the Brenner a few hours later. They had landed on Lampedusa two weeks earlier, and had no intention of staying in Italy. They wanted to reach relatives and find a job in Sweden. Just like Salvio wanted to reach his sister and find a job in Germany. He was taken aback by how desperate they looked and how young they were, so far away from home in search of a better life. As the three of them were standing in the waiting room together, they were not very different from each other at all, despite their vastly different backgrounds and ages – all of them were stranded in the middle of the Alps, following their hopes and dreams.

When that evening's Munich-bound train arrived with snow swirling down from its roof onto the platform, Salvio bid the young Eritreans farewell, assuring them not to worry if they got in trouble with the police – he could call a Carabinieri officer who was a friend of his back home. The look in his eyes was of compassion and sympathy; a complete turn-around from the disdain with which he referred to the criminal foreigners who he thought had taken his money. I can only hope that similar encounters will change other people's opinions of migrants as well, and I can only encourage people to talk *to* migrants instead of just talking *about* them.

\*\*\*

## The witch doctor's sacrifice and other stories

There are countless tales of fortune and misfortune that illustrate the necessity of revising Europe's migration laws and improving reception conditions. Practically everyone I met at the Brenner had good reasons to leave their home countries – and Italy as well. I've already described several cases, but there are some more worth sharing.

Perhaps the most shocking story I heard was that of Jabril, a 19 year-old Gambian young man, who was very upbeat and energetic despite the deeply disturbing circumstances he left behind. Jabril's father died when he was a child, and his step-father was given custody of him when his mother passed away as well. Jabril's step-father was a so-called Marabout, a witch doctor. Animism and voodoo are practiced in some parts of Gambia, and Marabouts are well-respected in several communities. One day, Jabril's step-father declared that the devil had told him he would be killed unless he sacrificed Jabril. His death was to take place in a ceremony, but Jabril's step-mother gave him some money and secretly encouraged him to escape before it took place.

Jabril fled to neighbouring Senegal. He spent a few months working there, and when he earned enough money, he travelled to Agadez, Niger – the gateway to Libya. He spent three months working as a construction worker in Agadez to pay his trip across the desert. He found another construction job in Libya, and his boss even treated him well, but he wanted to leave as soon as he saved enough money due to the frequent robberies and high risk of getting kidnapped. He crossed the Mediterranean one and a half years after leaving Gambia. Jabril was rescued at sea and taken to a reception centre in the southern Italian city of Taranto, which he described as dirty and overcrowded with hundreds of other migrants. He decided to leave due to the poor conditions and difficulty of communicating, since no one apparently spoke English there. He had heard from others who had left the centre that people in Germany speak English, and that it is possible to go to school there (which he had never been to but badly wanted to do), so he left the centre and headed north.

The inadequate reception conditions that pushed Jabril to leave Taranto, and so many others to leave Sicily, are not a phenomenon strictly confined to southern Italy. The experience a young man from Mali described to me proved that northern Italy's reception capabilities reached the breaking point a long time ago as well. The young man showed me a document he received in September 2014 from the Questura in Milan, inviting him to an initial asylum interview in November 2015. The sheer number of applications caused a waiting period of over a year for him to state his case. Owing to poor conditions and unemployment in Milan, he chose to try his luck in Germany.

Of course, due to its geographical proximity to Africa, Sicily is burdened with far more than its fair share of refugees, and the reception conditions I kept hearing about consistently painted a picture of particularly evident squalor. A group of Nigerians that had fled Boko Haram attacks in northern Nigeria told me that they decided to leave a reception centre in Sicily after seven months due to poor conditions and no progress with their asylum applications. A young man named Kalu, who seemed to be the leader of the group, complained about the quality of food at the centre, and about the fact that it was very isolated. The nearest place they could go to buy a phone card to call their relatives was a one hour walk away. Kalu also had trouble receiving medical care. He asked to see a doctor because he had strong abdominal pain that wouldn't go away, but the doctor simply told him that nothing was wrong with him. Kalu knew about the death of a Gambian refugee who hadn't received proper medical attention in a different Sicilian reception centre a few months earlier, and decided to head north to Germany rather than follow the same fate.

Kalu and his friends weren't alone in their discontent. Their reception centre made the headlines of local newspapers in September 2014, when refugees housed there protested their conditions. The facility is located literally in the middle of nowhere in the Sicilian province of Trapani, almost equidistant between the towns of Salemi to the south and Vita to the north, each about 3.5 km away. Some of the centre's refugees blocked the main road connecting Salemi and Vita by laying and sitting down across it, while others did the same near a school on another road. According to an eyewitness' post on social media that day, some exasperated locals almost ran over the protesting refugees with their cars. It was not the first time that refugees in the area protested their conditions by blocking roads.

Exasperation was also on display at the Brenner from time to time, but with less dangerous potential outcomes. On the same day the Nigerians passed through, a train conductor's outburst highlighted the frustrations that train personnel endure on a daily basis as a result of the constant stream of migrants heading north. Just as the day's 16:00 Munich-bound train was about to depart with a slight delay, four young Eritreans ran to the front of the train from a corner of the platform, opened the door to the first class wagon, hurried inside and locked themselves in the toilet, as a group of elderly passengers watched them board with suspicion. Infuriated, the German train conductor standing outside loudly snarled: "This situation here just makes me want to vomit!" and blew his whistle extra loudly to signal the train's departure.

On a different day, a tall Nigerian man with a bad leg created a scene at the Brenner because he refused to get off one of the international trains. The trilateral patrol warned the man that he would be arrested in Innsbruck if he didn't get off at the Brenner, but he protested angrily and told them they were wrong about their claim that he wasn't allowed to leave Italy. His attitude clearly didn't help him in any way, and only caused two more police officers to arrive at the platform, and another two observed from a distance. Finally, when the train was about to leave, he gave up, and got off, visibly raging in fury.

Unlike the stubborn Nigerian, a group of Syrians in their late 30s I met at the Brenner tried their best to keep a low profile, and were probably the most cautious travellers I had encountered thus far. They had every reason to be careful – and every reason to leave Italy. The group consisted of a couple with a 4 year-old girl and two men who became friends in Libya before crossing the Mediterranean together. The couple arrived in Italy in November 2014, and wanted to seek asylum in Switzerland. They managed to reach it, and stayed in a Swiss reception centre for three months, but were then sent back to Italy as a Dublin case. The couple was determined not to raise their child in Italy, so they decided to try seeking asylum in Germany. They met the two Syrian friends by chance in Milan's train station, where they were all cheated out of their money by a Tunisian man who took advantage of their lack of orientation and language skills. The man sold them train tickets to Germany for 300 Euros each – a hefty mark-up that the Syrians only realized when they saw the actual ticket price printed on the tickets they were given.

The young family left the Brenner before the two friends did because they thought they would be less likely to be checked by police without two other Syrians onboard. The two friends, Ahmad and Sayyid, ended up staying at the Brenner the whole day, since they didn't want to take trains which various groups of Africans who kept showing up at the Brenner were getting on. The Syrians thought that the police would be more likely to check them as a result of the many black faces onboard. I could understand all of their worries, but I didn't think that a veiled woman with a tattered suitcase, dishevelled-looking husband and child would look any less suspicious to police without the presence of other refugees onboard, while the two friends could have been mistaken for southern Europeans – one of them even had blue eyes. Nevertheless, their enduring presence at the Brenner allowed me to get to know them better than the couple, and both of them were very friendly.

Ahmad looked slightly older and spoke better English, while Sayyid, with the blue eyes, tried his best to communicate with a handful of words and a lot of gesturing. Ahmad was from Damascus and left the city when bombings and attacks made life there too dangerous for him and his wife and three children. They all fled to Turkey, where Ahmad found work as a butcher, which was also his profession in Syria. Despite the fact that he had a job, he didn't want to stay in Turkey because he was worried about his children's education. Although they were allowed to go to school, the curriculum was only in Turkish, and no effort was made to help them understand the lessons.

As soon as Ahmad saved enough money to send his wife and kids to Europe, he let them go ahead together with his brother. After a year in Turkey, Ahmad had enough money for his own trip, and flew to Libya, where he met Sayyid. Sayyid had fled directly to Libya earlier and worked as a shoemaker there, but wanted to leave after he was held for ransom by local bandits for the third time. As soon as he earned enough to pay smugglers, he decided to take a boat to Italy. Both he and Ahmad were at the Brenner six days after crossing the Mediterranean together.

Ahmad and Sayyid hadn't eaten a proper meal since leaving Sicily, so we all had lunch together in the flat. I asked them about their plans while they were wolfing down their pasta. Ahmad wanted to reach his wife and children, who were staying with distant relatives in Germany. They were lying low, waiting for him to join them so that they could officially request asylum together. Sayyid wanted to join his brother in Denmark, who was waiting for him in Copenhagen.

After lunch, we all sat down to watch TV until the next train arrived. I discovered that Sayyid had an impressive knowledge of football when a news segment about some football-related corruption scandal in Italy triggered a conversation about European teams. When that was over, Ahmad and Sayyid flipped through Italian and German-language channels incomprehensible to them until they ended up watching an episode of the American teen drama series *The O.C.* dubbed in Italian. They couldn't understand a word, but were transfixed. As they watched scenes with scantily-clad girls wrapping themselves around teenaged guys in the Californian suburbs, lesbians kissing and women drinking whiskey while smoking cigars, I could only imagine what they were thinking of the West, and of the fact that their children would soon become part of it.

# Part 3: Sicily, the Gateway to Europe

I felt slightly seasick. The windowless room I was sitting in was swaying with waves I couldn't see. As it swayed from side to side, the room creaked and the floor vibrated in tune with the ship's droning engine. A faint smell of exhaust fumes hung in the stale air. I decided to go outside. The crescent moon illuminated a choppy swath of the Mediterranean Sea. I held the guardrail tightly as the chilly wind whipped across the deck. Out on the horizon, far ahead, I could see the lights of another ship floating atop Europe's moat. Somewhere beyond the horizon was Sicily – the southern tip of the Promised Continent.

I thought of all the migrants I met at the Brenner; almost every one of them passed through the island on their way north, risking their lives to set foot on European soil. Now I myself was en route to Sicily's shores, but I was heading south, on an overnight ferry from Naples to Palermo. After hearing so many things about Sicily from refugees who got a less than warm welcome to Europe there, I decided to investigate further in person. I wanted to understand how bad conditions in reception centres really are, and whether the stories I heard from recent arrivals that had never even been to a reception centre were isolated cases or part of a wider trend.

# Palermo

Palermo was the first stop of my exploratory visit to Sicily. Arriving in this chaotic, multicultural city felt like coming to a foreign country. Palm trees, Arab and Byzantine architecture, shouting street vendors and extensive open markets give the city an exotic flair. Adding to the feeling of being abroad is the local dialect, which was barely comprehensible to me although I speak Italian fluently. It is a place where Europe meets Africa and the Middle East in the past and present. Over the course of its rich history dating back to 736 B.C., Palermo has been under Phoenician, Greek, Carthaginian, Roman, Byzantine, Arab, Norman, Spanish and finally Italian rule, with some interludes of still other foreign control. Today, the city is a kaleidoscope of historic influences and current inhabitants from around the world.

Palermo's rich history stands in contrast to its relative poverty compared to the rest of Italy and Western Europe. Crumbling buildings, beggars and people searching through rubbish containers were a common sight as I walked along poorly paved alleyways choked with the smell of moped exhaust. Many of the apparently homeless were dark-skinned, but not everyone. Nationalities from Ghana to Bangladesh were represented along with some locals at a food bank operated by the Caritas I visited. Most of the people I spoke to had been in Palermo for many years, with no prospect of improving their situation. Unlike the refugees I met at the Brenner, these migrants seemed somehow resigned to their fate. They didn't have the energy and determination that those en route to Germany had shown time and time again. Perhaps they lost both after years of misfortune. Or perhaps they were never as driven, and ended up in perpetual misery as a result.

The starkest contrast I witnessed in Palermo was on the steps of an intricately sculpted church's facade overlooking a beautiful piazza in front of an equally impressive city hall building. I walked up the steps to take a picture of the breathtaking architecture, and saw a black man eating the contents of a bag of food I recognized to be one of those distributed by the Caritas. I approached the man, but quickly realized that having a conversation with him would be difficult. He slurred his words and his bloodshot eyes would rarely meet mine; all I could understand was that he was from Ghana and had been in Palermo for four years, interrupted by a few months in Milan which apparently didn't help. As I started to leave, he pointed to the sky and said "Jesus is number one", and that Jesus wanted me to stay there and talk to him. He had gone mad. Just like the brother of Abubacar, the young man from Guinea-Bissau I met at the Brenner who went to visit his ailing sibling.

While Palermo has its share of visible desperation, there are also positive stories to tell. I visited one of the very few reception centres in Sicily that welcome visitors, and found a clean, well-functioning operation complete with language courses, after-school homework assistance for children, volunteer doctors and counsellors. Part of the facility provided housing for asylum-seekers while other daytime-only services were available for anyone who showed up in need. Over the course of the centre's 14-year history, over 7,000 individuals and families registered with the facility. I spoke to two men from Côte d'Ivoire there who confirmed my impressions: the centre worked well and they were more or less content. Their main concern (and soon the main topic of our conversation) was the political situation in their home country, which they were trying to influence from abroad through an organization that one of them founded.

*** 

## Reception hell and heaven in Salemi

After visiting Palermo, I drove south-west to a reception centre I knew definitely wasn't a success story: the centre that Kalu, the Nigerian I spoke to at the Brenner, decided to leave together with a few others after they blocked local streets to protest their living conditions. After some searching, I finally found the centre hidden behind vegetation just off of the main provincial road connecting Vita and Salemi, the closest towns in the area. Isolation is almost an understatement; the centre is absolutely remote, and leaving it on foot means walking along the dangerous provincial road which has no sidewalk and is full of blind turns. From the outside, the two storey building looked rather old and run down; its outer walls were discoloured with mildew stains and unevenly fading paint. Nevertheless, majestic pine trees and palmettos surrounding the property suggested that it was once a respectable residence. I walked to the front gate of the facility, which led into a gravel courtyard, hoping to be able to talk to someone without going inside, since I knew I wouldn't be welcome by the centre's staff.

An Indian-looking man I later learned was from Bangladesh approached me, and I asked him if he spoke English. He said no, but pointed me to a group of Africans sitting down in plastic garden chairs in the courtyard. I hesitated to step inside, but the Africans motioned for me to come in, so I entered the courtyard and sat down with them. I spoke to two Gambians who were playing checkers on an old set with some missing chips replaced with bottle caps. They assured me that no staff was around; they only came to serve lunch and dinner (though by law, reception centres need to be staffed all the time).

The Gambians had a long list of complaints about the centre and the lack of progress with their asylum applications. They had both been in the centre for 10 months (the regular maximum stay should be 3 months, and up to 6 months in exceptional cases), but hadn't even had their asylum interview yet. They told me that they went to the local Questura on more than one occasion to inquire about their asylum procedure, but weren't let inside. They told me that some of the others in the centre (30 in total, coming from Gambia, Ghana, Nigeria and Bangladesh) had been there even longer without being interviewed by the asylum commission.

According to the Gambians, the centre itself was poorly maintained and poorly managed. They told me that the heating didn't work all winter and was only fixed in late February. After it was fixed, it was only turned on for two hours every evening from 6 to 8 o'clock. The food was often prepared a day or two in advance and made almost everyone feel sick. Just like Kalu, the Gambians and others at the centre also had abdominal pain and were also not treated by local doctors, who only gave them painkillers. If bad food weren't enough, they also thought that the water, which they said came from a well in the courtyard, was contaminated.

Every time the refugees complained to the centre's management, they were told that they could leave if they didn't like it. Nothing improved, so the migrants protested, making the headlines I had read before. The Gambians stopped blocking roads to protest their conditions after a while because it didn't change anything and because they didn't want to disrespect the local population, even if they themselves felt disrespected. At the end of our conversation, I asked whether they would consider leaving Italy because of their conditions. To my astonishment, the Gambians said that despite everything, they liked Italy and wanted to stay.

After my sobering conversation with the Gambians, I decided to leave the centre before any staff showed up, and went to another reception centre I knew existed in nearby Salemi. Upon entering the compact hilltop town with tight streets and beautiful views of the Sicilian countryside, I immediately noticed the large number of Africans and Bangladeshis/Pakistanis walking around. The reception centre I wanted to reach was much easier to find than the previous one, thanks to street signs still indicating its former use: a three star hotel. In fact, it was a large and rather well known hotel in the area, but became a reception centre when the prospect of full year-round occupancy became a lucrative alternative to increasingly weak tourist seasons. In contrast to the small and shabby centre I had just visited before, the former hotel was large and looked decent.

I met three Gambians and a Libyan-born half-Somali/half-Malian Tuareg just outside the property's front gate, and asked them how they liked it. In stark contrast to my previous encounter, they had no complaints about the centre – the food was ok, the heating worked and the staff was friendly. Indeed, while we were talking, several staff members came and left the centre, and one of the Gambians greeted them very warmly. However, the Tuareg told me that he hadn't been properly treated for a gunshot wound in his leg, and wanted to go elsewhere simply for medical care. He had been in the centre for over a year.

The Gambians' main concern was the status of their asylum application. Two of them had been at the centre for a year and three months, and had still not seen the asylum commission for their interview. The third Gambian had only been there two months, but hadn't even been fingerprinted yet. No one at the centre was in a position to help them with their asylum application, so all they could do is wait. Unlike the previous reception centre, which had no recreational facilities at all for the migrants to pass the time, this centre had a football field and the Gambians told me there were many other activities at the centre, as well as the possibility of hanging around town. In fact, they were on their way to the supermarket, to spend their 2.50 Euro per day pocket money.

\*\*\*

## Siculiana and Porto Empedocle

My next stop after Salemi was another former hotel turned into a reception centre in the town of Siculiana, near Porto Empedocle, one of the main ports of arrival for migrants. Siculiana is a picturesque hilltop town similar to Salemi, but the situation I found there was yet again vastly different. I was planning on talking to migrants in front of the facility, as I had done before, but I knew I couldn't follow through with my plan the moment I drove onto the parking lot. A group of Carabinieri officers were standing outside the centre's entrance and a Carabinieri van with barred windows was parked outside. The officers told me I couldn't park there, and I played the tourist, saying that I was looking for a place to eat lunch (which I actually was planning to do afterwards). One of the officers directed me to a nearby restaurant, which I went to. A police van was parked outside, and inside, two groups of police officers were finishing lunch. For a small town of a few thousand residents, the police presence here was remarkable.

After lunch, I went into town to see if I could find some migrants I could talk to on the street. Unlike Salemi, which was full of them, no migrants were to be seen. I went into a local bar and asked the barman about the centre and how it was seen by the local population. He told me that there wasn't much interaction with the refugees, who mainly stayed in the centre and rarely came into town. He said there had never been any problems with the refugees, but some residents were suspicious of them nevertheless. I asked him about the heavy police presence and he assumed it was simply a precautionary measure.

On my way out of town, police standing on the side of the road waved me over to check my documents. They were friendly, but beyond checking my documents, they also asked me what I was doing in Sicily. My enthusiastic account of my holiday thus far satisfied the officers, but as I drove off, I could clearly tell something was fishy. That much police in such a small town made absolutely no sense, except for one reason: to prevent people like me from being too nosy around that particular reception centre.

The next day, I visited Porto Empedocle on the off-chance that I might meet newly arrived refugees who were simply disembarked without further ado, as I had heard about at the Brenner. Porto Empedocle is a compact town on a steep hill leading down to a relatively large port area serving a number of small boats, medium-sized fishing vessels, cargo ships and ferries – including the only ferry service to Lampedusa. Apart from its main pedestrian street, the town is run-down and quite unappealing. I saw many abandoned buildings, and many more inhabited ones in urgent need of renovation. A massive oil power plant stands on the shore next to the sprawling port, slightly hidden behind a hill, and smokestacks frame the other side of town. As I stood on one of the docks overlooking the harbour, I thought of all the migrants who had arrived here after being rescued by the Italian Coast Guard or transferred on the ferry from Lampedusa. This was the first bit of Europe they saw. Surely disappointing, and sadly, for many of them, the beginning of a long stretch of further disappointments.

I didn't see any refugees wandering around or living in the abandoned buildings while I was there, but I did meet a Nigerian who was begging in front of a supermarket on the outskirts of town. He told me that he had arrived four years ago and was brought to a reception centre in Catania, on Sicily's eastern coast. After waiting a year and a half there for his asylum application to be processed, he decided to give up on getting regularized and left the centre. He moved to Agrigento, the capital of the province Porto Empedocle is located in, with a few others, and has been trying to survive off of begging ever since. He told me that he wants to go back to Nigeria, since he realizes that he is wasting his life begging on the streets, but wants to wait a few years until Boko Haram is no longer a threat.

\*\*\*

## Friendly nuns and hungry refugees in Agrigento

Agrigento is a much nicer and bigger town than Porto Empedocle, and is impressively situated atop an elongated hill not far from the sea. The town itself and nearby ruins of Greek temples, a UNESCO World Heritage Site, attract thousands of tourists every year. Agrigento is also the home of many newly arrived and more established migrants from all over Africa. The more established ones typically make a living selling everything from key chains to trainers in markets and on street corners, while the newly arrived migrants usually either live in reception centres or lead a precarious existence outside of them.

I visited a canteen run by local nuns, which serves free food to those in need every day, in order to talk to migrants and learn more about the conditions they face. The canteen's nuns and volunteers were extremely warm and welcoming, and told me that it operates entirely through volunteer work and donations. The local government doesn't contribute at all, but local politicians show up with flowers for photo opportunities from time to time, showing false solidarity for positive newspaper articles. The canteen is open to anyone, and they even offer a pork-free option for Muslims. Indeed, I saw a wide range of nationalities there, ranging from Africa to the Middle East and beyond, including some Italians.

After talking to the nuns and volunteers, I struck up a very friendly conversation with two young refugees, Karamo from Gambia and Malam from Guinea-Bissau, who had just finished eating lunch there. They were both only 18 years old. Karamo landed on Lampedusa one and a half years ago and was transferred to Agrigento, where he became friends with Malam, who had also just arrived. They lived in the same reception centre until Malam received a residence permit for humanitarian reasons and had to leave the centre as a result. Since he didn't have a job to support himself, he stayed with friends in Agrigento and depended on the canteen and his friends' help to sustain himself. Karamo was still in the centre because he received his residence permit later, and still had two months left before he had to leave the centre as well. In the meantime, he could complete his Middle School diploma, for which he was attending evening classes.

Facing impending homelessness, Karamo planned on leaving Agrigento to find a job somewhere in Italy as soon as he was kicked out. He had worked as a bricklayer in Libya before crossing the Mediterranean, and already made a round of Sicily's main towns and cities to look for a construction job, but wasn't successful. Despite the difficulties on the horizon, Karamo struck me as very upbeat, energetic and intelligent, and he told me that I was the friendliest European he had met so far. In fact, he even invited me to come to his reception centre to read a story he had written – a fellow writer, of course we would click.

I followed him through Agrigento's tight streets and alleys to a small apartment building that looked just like the others in the neighbourhood. We stepped inside, and he led me up a flight of stairs to his room. The interior of the building was in good condition and clean apart from some untidiness; his room was rather small and had four beds and a table, but the walls were freshly painted and the room had a balcony, which his roommates were sitting on while chatting and listening to music. After an initial moment of visible suspicion on their part, the ice was broken and we talked about their situations. They had all been there at least a year; one of them had been there for two. They said that except for the food and the long wait for their documents, the centre was ok. Karamo told me that he had gone to the canteen to eat lunch because he didn't like the reception centre's food, and indeed, I spotted an uneaten plate of spaghetti on the table.

Karamo's story was a love story full of hardship. It was surprisingly well written, and ended with a young couple's hope of moving to America. The male character was named Marco, my own first name; a memorable coincidence at the end of a memorable encounter. I gave Karamo some money, wished him well, and left the centre with my head so full of thoughts that I hardly noticed my surroundings for a few minutes. Would the young man find a way to success? I truly hoped he would beat the odds.

*** 

## Caltanissetta's Pakistani community

After visiting Agrigento, I drove inland to Caltanissetta, in central Sicily. The visibly low-income town is not typically on tourist itineraries and has a reputation as being a mafia stronghold, but I went to visit a reception centre I had heard was particularly large and important for the region. The centre is located on the outskirts of town in an impenetrable complex that looks like a maximum-security prison. Part of it is also a prison of sorts: foreigners with an expulsion order are detained in an extra high-security section of the facility prior to their forcible removal from Italy. Tall fences surround the compound, and the property is heavily guarded not only by the police and Carabinieri, but even the military. Signs posted on the perimeter fences state that filming and photography are forbidden.

I approached the centre on foot, hoping to be able to talk to some migrants who might be outside. Indeed, there were many standing and sitting just outside the entrance, and I sat down with a group of talkative Pakistanis who were just out of sight from the soldiers guarding the front gate. Most of them had been in the centre for over a year and were released once they got a residence permit, but since they couldn't find a job, they became homeless and camped out in the area. Most of them were there that day to renew their expiring or already expired residence permits (all granted for humanitarian reasons), and showed me in frustration that they were only given an appointment up to six months away – therefore putting them in a prolonged limbo that would make it impossible for them to find anything other than illegal employment at best.

The group described the centre as a business. They said the staff is reasonably courteous and the food is ok, but pocket money is given in the form of electronic keys that can only be used to buy drinks, sweets and cigarettes from vending machines inside the centre. Migrants are housed inside containers in the compound – 15 in each one. They said the toilets are problematic, and fights among refugees frequently brake out as a result of their living conditions and the mental stress of living in uncertainty for months on end. They all agreed that the quality of service gradually deteriorated while they were in the centre.

One of the Pakistanis in the group was still in the centre and had been there for slightly over a year, while another member of the group had arrived in the area three weeks ago, wanted to enter the centre, but was turned away because there was no space for him. I was somewhat puzzled by this, since I assumed that he had been rescued at sea and was at least given the chance to claim asylum in Italy if he chose to, but found out that he – as well as most of the others – had not come by boat at all. Almost everyone in the group had come to Italy via the land route through Turkey, Greece, the Balkans and Austria. I couldn't understand why they would choose to come all the way to Sicily when they could have requested asylum anywhere else, and their response was that getting documents in Sicily, especially at Caltanissetta's reception centre, was easier than anywhere else they knew of. Apparently, word of this has spread far and wide among the Pakistani community; I saw a far more Pakistanis in Caltanissetta than anywhere else I visited.

While talking to the Pakistanis, I soon found myself chatting mainly with one particularly friendly and talkative man named Mohammad. He left Pakistan when the Taliban attacked his clothing shop in Lahore, possibly because his brother was in the military, and made it all the way to Caltanissetta's reception centre, where he spent one year and two months. After getting his residence permit, he went to Milan to look for a job but couldn't find one. After six months of searching there, he went to Paris and found work as a painter and construction worker for three months. He spent three more months there looking for another job but couldn't find any. By this time, his residence permit had expired, so he made his way back down to Caltanissetta to renew it and hope the local job market had improved.

Sadly for Mohammad, neither the job market nor the waiting time for his residence permit renewal was going in his favour. With no money left from his job in Paris, he camped out near the centre with some other Pakistanis, and took me there to show me his living conditions. He and a few others lived in tents or makeshift shelters on the second floor of an abandoned construction site only a five minute walk down the street from the reception centre. The skeletal building had a roof, two floors and vertical supporting columns, but no walls. The tents and shelters made of scrap wood and cardboard were all in a corner of the building's concrete floor, which was strewn with bricks and construction debris.

Perhaps the most shocking and simultaneously humbling thing to me was how Mohammad told me they managed to feed themselves: refugees inside the reception centre gave them food and water from their own rations. Solidarity between fellow refugees allowed these people to survive.

\*\*\*

## Mineo, Europe's largest refugee business

Europe's largest reception centre was the next stop on my tour of Sicily. The centre is located in a sparsely populated area in eastern Sicily's interior, amidst citrus groves and grass fields. Mineo, the nearest town, is 9 km away on a hilltop several hundred metres above the surrounding countryside. The sprawling compound comprises around 200 buildings and interloping roads which in its entirety resemble an American-style subdivision. Indeed, it was originally built to house US military personnel and their families, who were stationed at nearby Sigonella NATO air base. In 2011, the facility was turned into a reception centre – officially to house 2,000 refugees, but is now home to almost double as many.

Mineo's reception centre made national headlines only a few weeks before I visited it. The centre was under investigation by both the local district anti-mafia commission as well as the district court for suspected embezzlement and corruption. Among those under investigation was Luca Odevaine, a high-ranking member of Rome's municipal government in charge of refugee accommodation. Mr. Odevaine was arrested in December 2014 on charges of manipulating migratory flows and tenders for Roman reception centres, but was also active in Sicily, and served as the commissioner for Mineo's operating contract's call for tender.[8] In March 2015, Italy's national anti-corruption authority confirmed that Mineo's call for tender was illegitimate, and investigations continued for a variety of other offenses including diversion of public funds destined

---

[8] For more information (in Italian), see:
http://www.panorama.it/news/cronaca/mineo-business-accoglienza-sotto-inchiesta/

for the centre but used to finance local festivals, shows and markets, as well as the employment of centre administrators' relatives, municipal councillors and unelected local political candidates.[9]

Well before I reached the centre, I saw several Africans walking or cycling along the provincial road (which has no sidewalk and barely any shoulder) it is located on. When the complex came into view, I was struck by its sheer size. Driving along its fenced perimeter, I passed rows upon rows of two-story houses, basketball courts, football fields and playgrounds full of men, women and children. Military trucks were parked in front of side entrances and the front entrance was guarded by the military, police and Carabinieri. I parked my car as others had along the road, and approached a group of African men sitting on the guardrail diagonally across the street from the main entrance.

I initially spoke to a Gambian, who told me he had been in the centre for a year and half. Before I could ask him more, an old minivan pulled up and everyone sitting on the guardrail except one got up and piled into it, including the Gambian, and they were off. The one who stayed behind was a soft-spoken Nigerian named Lawrence who explained that the minivan's driver used to live in the centre and had since received his residence permit. He made money by driving migrants still there

---

[9] More information (in Italian) is available at:
http://www.ilgiornale.it/news/politica/cara-mineo-garantiti-posti-lavoro-ai-parenti-coi-soldi-i-1108983.html

to and from Catania, the nearest bigger city, charging five Euros per person. In other words, he ran an illegal taxi service. Lawrence wasn't outside to wait for the driver like the others, but rather in the hope of finding a job for the day. He told me that local farmers sometimes come by to look for day labourers to work in the orange and lemon groves, and pay 20 Euros for a full day of work – black, of course.

Lawrence had been in the reception centre for a year and five months, and said the conditions were poor. Quarters are cramped – each building houses 18-19 migrants, four or five to each room, including the kitchens, which are stripped of their appliances and used as bedrooms. There are only two toilets per building and it is up to the migrants to clean the interiors themselves, so inevitably there is conflict. Lawrence told me that fights break out relatively frequently, but the police and military don't intervene. They only deal with any injuries caused by an incident.

The biggest problem according to Lawrence is the food. Migrants are given either rice with vegetable stew or pasta, and meat (always chicken) is only served once per week. He told me that many migrants get stomach cramps because of the food and when they visit a doctor, they're only given painkillers. Lawrence told me that he and many others don't eat the centre's food anymore. Instead, they buy food outside of the centre and cook it inside their rooms on portable electric stoves they also buy outside. However, bringing meat and canned goods into the centre is forbidden – an obstacle that is circumvented regularly by creative smuggling techniques and friends passing food through the fence when no one is looking.

Financing the external food supply, as well as clothing which is also not adequately provided, is a challenge that has led many migrants like Lawrence to ask relatives back home to send them money. Making matters worse, and completely against established regulations, the pocket money the migrants are entitled to by law is given in the form of one pack of cigarettes every two days – completely useless to non-smokers like Lawrence, who can't even sell the unused cigarettes easily outside the centre because of its isolation. Unavoidably, a few relatively better-off refugees have taken advantage of the situation, buying food in bulk outside of the centre and selling it to others inside at a mark-up.

I asked Lawrence whether he was at least able to learn some Italian despite the difficulties, so that he could improve his chances of getting a job once he got out. Even that was a problem at the centre. He told me that language classes are held three times per week, but the instructors only speak Italian and are not able to translate or explain anything in English, so most migrants stop attending classes after the first few sessions. Lawrence had only attended one.

After my chat with Lawrence, I headed up the hill to Mineo, which is a sleepy hilltop town that only a handful of migrants venture up to due to the distance and steep climb. From the town, the reception centre looks like an island of brown-orange roofs immersed in green, far below in the distance. There could hardly be a more visual depiction of the vast difference between the migrants' depressing reality in the lowlands, and the locals' quiet haven atop their lofty perch, partially financed by the money stolen by corrupt officials.

***

## Pozzallo, Syracuse and Augusta

The next stop of my trip was Pozzallo, located on the south-eastern edge of Sicily. Along with Porto Empedocle, it is one of the main ports of arrival for migrants rescued by the Italian Coast Guard. Pozzallo is a tourist town with turquoise-blue water and sandy beaches, and makes for a much nicer first glimpse of the Promised Continent than Porto Empedocle. Its port is on the edge of town, out of sight from the centre, and there are no smoke stacks looming nearby. The port is slightly smaller than Porto Empedocle's, but also has docks for cargo ships and a ferry service to Malta. I first spotted a large Coast Guard facility and Coast Guard ships in the middle of the marina, and as I walked toward the ferry loading dock, my heart skipped a beat. Behind a fence, in between stacked cargo containers, dozens of dilapidated boats and small ships with Arabic inscriptions on their bows were lying on their sides on the dock. These were the smugglers' relics.

As I walked along the fence to get a closer look, I felt chills run down my spine. The boats and ships were all made of wood, their faded paint was cracking and some were badly damaged. On some of the ships tilting in my direction, I saw clothing and water canisters scattered across the main deck. Around a corner, up against the wall of a small building, was a pile of life jackets. Amidst the ship graveyard, right by the fence further up the perimeter road, I saw a large, deflated raft on the ground. I was close to tears as I thought about the hundreds who were likely packed on that raft and left to their destinies out at sea. I wondered whether everyone had been rescued, or whether some or all had drowned before help arrived.

I didn't see any newly arrived refugees in Pozzallo, but did talk to a Nigerian man who was begging near the main town square. He told me that he had arrived in Lampedusa three years ago, and spent one year and two months in a reception centre in Catania before getting a residence permit for humanitarian reasons. He told me that his wife had just had a baby, but he didn't have a job so he badly needed money to feed his young family. I gave him some money, and left Pozzallo with a heavy heart.

Syracuse, a very scenic, historically important town on Sicily's east coast, was my next stop. The town's Greek ruins and baroque architecture give it an elegant atmosphere, and unsurprisingly, it's a tourist magnet. Syracuse also has a relatively large reception centre, which is another example of the isolation that appears to be typical of refugee accommodation in Sicily. The centre is located far away from the touristic centre, in a residential area at the very edge of town, tucked away at the end of a dead-end street, hidden behind an empty lot of overgrown weeds and a row of trees.

I approached the centre on foot, hoping as always to talk to migrants outside, but none were around. As I got closer, I saw that a Carabinieri patrol car was parked by the entrance with officers inside, and decided to turn around. Unlike the centre in Siculiana, I had no touristic excuses to be there – there was practically no way to end up there by accident; it was simply too far out of the way from anything else. I even had trouble finding it. I walked around the neighbourhood for a few minutes in the hope of running into a centre resident leaving or coming back to it, but didn't see any, and left.

Situated about 30 km further up the coast from Syracuse is the port of Augusta, the third main point of arrival for migrants rescued at sea. Augusta is a bustling port town on a thin peninsula which hosts a large Italian Navy base. Several gray Navy ships and even a few submarines line one side of the peninsula, while barracks occupy a good portion of the slender strip of land. I noticed a few Africans while exploring the town and spoke to a young Nigerian who was begging in front of a supermarket. He told me that he had arrived in Augusta 11 months ago, and spent six months in a reception centre there, but the centre was closed and he was transferred to a centre in Città Giardino, a small town just north of Syracuse, right by a massive oil refinery. He told me he was almost 19 when he arrived but told the authorities he was two years younger in order to increase his chances of being able to stay – well knowing that unaccompanied minors get special treatment and can't be deported.

According to the Nigerian, the conditions at both the centre in Augusta and in Città Giardino were not great, but acceptable. However, food was a problem, which he attributed to the vastly different type of food that he was used to eating in Africa. He also told me that he never received any pocket money, which led him to return to Augusta to beg in front of the supermarket from time to time, as he was doing that day. He also missed being in Augusta because he felt that the people there are much friendlier than in Città Giardino. Indeed, as we spoke in front of the supermarket, locals constantly came by and gave him money or an item they had just bought.

Despite the difficulties and uncertain future the young Nigerian was facing, he refused to complain. As I referred to his reception conditions rather critically, he said that they were simply something to get used to. He was thankful for being in Italy and didn't want to jeopardize his stay in any way. Perhaps he felt that he pushed his luck already enough by getting the authorities to believe he was underage when in reality he wasn't, but in any case, his humble attitude was quite remarkable.

The same day I was in Augusta, unknown to me at the time, a rescue operation was underway at sea that would bring new arrivals to Augusta. According to a local newspaper, 389 refugees mainly from Eritrea, Syria and Pakistan landed there later that day, and a Tunisian smuggler was arrested. Over 1,000 more migrants were rescued in other rescue operations around Sicily that weekend. Migrants were brought to all the ports I had visited a few days before: Pozzallo, Porto Empedocle and Augusta, as well as Lampedusa. I had heard that Catania's train station is the main gateway to the north for newly arrived migrants who want to leave Sicily immediately, so I hoped to accompany some of them on my own way back home. I had also heard that an Italian-Moroccan woman who lives in Catania helps migrants passing through there, and was eager to meet her.

\*\*\*

## The Angels of Catania

Catania is Sicily's second biggest city after Palermo and also has a large, bustling port. Its location on the coast at the foot of Mt. Etna is spectacular, and I enjoyed some sightseeing both in the city and around Mt. Etna before my departure. The city is very multicultural and has large African and Pakistani communities like Palermo, but it appeared to have fewer beggars than its larger sibling. Nevertheless, living conditions for migrants are very basic, as those who don't live in reception centres are typically housed in run-down apartments in poorer neighbourhoods. Peeking into some of the dimly-lit interiors, I saw very cramped quarters and rudimentary cooking facilities – sometimes even only basic outdoor grills in courtyards.

On the day I planned to leave, I went to the train station and immediately spotted a group of likely refugees – Arab-looking men who were talking in excited voices in a corner of the main hall that smelled strongly of body odour. I approached them, and indeed, they were Syrian refugees. Outside, another group of Syrians were talking to an Italian girl who seemed to be giving them information of some sort, so I went to her and introduced myself. She told me that her name was Anna and that she worked together with Nour, the Italian-Moroccan I had heard about, who joined us a little while later.

Anna and Nour are exceptional people that deserve the highest possible praise. The two young ladies in their late 20s help newly arrived refugees seeking to head north on an almost daily basis, completely on their own and completely voluntarily. They're not part of any organization, get no funding and receive barely any support from the local community, but despite the obstacles they face, they help thousands upon thousands of migrants leave Sicily to pursue a better future elsewhere. Nour is the duo's leader, and is a very tough, energetic, no-nonsense type of person while

Anna is a gentler character who provides valuable support.

Nour's fluent Arabic and strong personality provide her with the tools to not only help, but inspire the many migrants seeking a better life. She is well known and respected throughout the Mediterranean and many migrants know about her before they even leave their home countries. She is often the person who refugees in distress at sea call from their boats for help, providing her with coordinates she relays to the Italian Coast Guard. Once they arrive in Catania, Nour and Anna provide the refugees with information about how to get to Milan, which is a final destination for some, and a convenient transit hub to other places for most. Beyond advising migrants about which trains to take to reach Milan, Nour and Anna help them buy Italian phone SIM cards or withdraw money sent from friends and family and even distribute a few items of clothing from donations they collect when there are no new arrivals.

The two angels of Catania are not only a humanitarian saviour for migrants, but also serve as an invaluable alternative to opportunists and smugglers who lurk around Catania's train station trying to take advantage of unwitting refugees. Anna told me that unscrupulous criminals often sell train tickets to migrants at many times their actual price, or even offer to smuggle them to other countries. Nour has had numerous run-ins with smugglers at the station who tried to lure migrants into expensive deals.

Unsurprisingly, the train station police have a friendly relationship with her and Anna.

The day I was at Catania's train station was an especially challenging one for Nour and Anna. Easter had just passed, and because of the holidays, all trains leaving Sicily were booked out for two full days. The 15-20 Syrians I initially saw soon became close to 50 refugees mainly from Syria, Eritrea and Sudan, all crowded around the station's front entrance. Anna told me that sometimes, literally hundreds show up in a single day, and getting them all on their way out of Catania can be a logistical nightmare even during off-peak travel times. Nour made periodic announcements explaining the situation in Arabic, and between the explanations, she made quick phone calls and visits to the ticket offices of various long distance bus companies located across the street from the train station. Because of the booked out trains, scheduled buses to Rome and other cities were also almost fully booked for the day, so the final solution Nour came up with was to hire an entire coach to bring around 50 people to Milan. I would be one of them.

The coach was to depart Catania between six and eight o'clock in the evening, so I spent the afternoon tagging along while Nour and Anna accompanied migrants to local shops where they could buy SIM cards and to money transfer agencies where they collected funds needed to continue their journeys. Anna told me about the various difficulties they face trying to help migrants, such as shop owners who reluctantly sell SIM cards to large groups because of the time it takes to activate them and the little to no money made, or the local Caritas which provides them with little help in the form of very limited food donations and infrequent access to shower facilities. She told me that they also tried to get help from Catania's mosque, but the people running it were unfriendly and reluctant to help migrants.

When I wasn't tagging along or chatting with Nour or Anna, I talked to migrants who were waiting for the coach to leave. Everyone I spoke to had arrived over Easter weekend, only two or three days earlier. None of them had been fingerprinted. The group of Syrians I had initially approached spent one night in a reception centre before they walked out of the centre along with several others the next morning, and made their way to Catania. They all wanted to go to Germany. A group of Eritreans who wanted to request asylum in England told me that in the reception centre they were taken to after disembarking, they were asked whether they had money. Those who had money were allowed to leave, while those who didn't had to stay.

Among the dozens of refugees waiting to leave that afternoon, there was also a Syrian young man who had arrived in Sicily seven months ago, made his way to Germany and got asylum status in six months. He was back in Catania to look for a friend of his who had just made the crossing. He hadn't heard from him since his friend left Libya, and was worried that he was dead. He planned to hang around Catania's train station for a few days to meet his friend if he was still alive, or at least hear news about him from possible survivors of the boat he was on, if there were any.

Shortly before departing Catania, I met a very friendly half-Syrian, half-Palestinian man named Akil who was also waiting for the coach to leave, and we quickly became friends. The coach was finally ready for us around 7 o'clock, by which time the refugees were eager to leave, as it was getting chilly outside. I sat next to Akil, and when everyone was inside, Nour stepped to the front of the coach, grabbed the microphone and gave a fiery speech in Arabic that energized the mainly Syrian passengers. At the end of her speech, the coach erupted in cheers and applause. Outside, Anna unravelled a revolutionary Syrian flag, to the Syrians' euphoric approval.

After Nour's farewell, I expected the coach to leave, but it remained parked for several minutes. After a while, she came back and explained that a young Eritrean no more than 20 years old I had noticed waiting with us earlier had snuck onboard (with her approval) without paying because he didn't have any money. The driver noticed when he counted heads before leaving, and refused to depart unless the young man either paid or got off. Nour's solution was to ask everyone who could to chip in some money to pay for his trip, and negotiated the price down to 80 Euros from the 110 everyone else had paid – a suspiciously high price that I can only interpret as the coach company taking advantage of the situation. It took less than a minute to collect enough money, and shortly thereafter, we were off.

As the coach left Catania, Middle Eastern music sounded from mobile phones, and mixed with the cheerful chatter and pungent smell of 50 men who had just crossed the Mediterranean Sea. It felt at once surreal to be among them, and at the same time, it felt oddly normal – after all, it was simply a group of otherwise ordinary people who had a long coach ride ahead of them. Pretty soon, some started snoring, others focused on their smart phones, and others listened to music. It only became once again evident that this was anything but an ordinary group of travellers when the coach reached the port of Messina, on Sicily's northeast coast, in order to board a ferry which would take us to mainland Italy. No one had ever been on a ferry before, and everyone was thoroughly impressed as the coach drove into the belly of the ship together with other vehicles.

Another unforgettable moment took place several hours later at a motorway rest area near Rome, shortly after sunrise. I was washing my hands in the toilet when the Eritrean who had no money came to the sink next to mine to do the same. He looked at me wash my hands as water flowed from the faucet, and then stretched his hands out without moving them, expecting water to flow like it did from mine, but none did. He did this several times, visibly perplexed, and I explained that he had to move his hands in front of the sensor in order for the water to flow. He smiled in thanks, and proceeded to wet his hands and feet, which in turn perplexed me. Shortly thereafter, I saw him on his knees, bending over forward and back, in a corner of the parking lot outside. Then I understood: he had wet his hands and feet as part of the Muslim ritual preceding prayer.

\*\*\*

## Akil's perilous journey from Syria to Sicily

During the long trip to Milan, Akil and I had many amicable conversations in which he told me his story and described what he had seen on his way to Europe. Akil was from Yarmouk, a suburb of Damascus which was established as a refugee camp for Palestinian refugees in 1957 and has been the home of Syria's largest Palestinian community ever since. He studied civil engineering and completed compulsory military service just as the opposition movement against Syrian President Bashar al-Assad started to turn violent. Akil barely avoided being selected to participate in a crackdown against the opposition in Homs shortly before being discharged from the military, but was soon recalled to service. Akil refused to go back to the military and kill his own people for Assad, so he kept a low profile in Yarmouk to evade the draft. Yarmouk became a rebel stronghold as Syria's civil war unfolded, and was bombed repeatedly from late 2011. Akil's family members fled to other parts of Damascus, but he decided to stay despite the danger. On one occasion, he was almost killed by a sniper right in front of his home. He was sitting on the floor outside to smoke, and bent down to light the coal of his hookah pipe. Just as he raised his head after lighting it, a bullet pelted into his leg, right above his knee. The sniper had been aiming for his head, and barely missed.

Akil lived in Yarmouk until one day in late 2012, when his mother refused to let him return after a visit. Shortly thereafter, the camp was besieged by government troops.[10] He couldn't return, but didn't want to stay with his parents, who to his dismay supported Assad. He never intended on leaving Syria, but one day, a childhood friend who lived in Dubai showed up with a flight ticket for him, and insisted that he come with him to start a new life there. Akil flew to Dubai, and spent one and a half years there working odd jobs while renewing his tourist visa on a month to month basis. Life in Dubai was tough. He made little money and had to spend almost everything he earned on visa extensions and the high cost of living there. He tried to obtain a residence permit but was constantly rejected, and when he lost his last job, he decided to leave.

Akil's final hope was to reach Europe. His uncle emigrated from Syria to Germany in the 1970s, and although Akil didn't get along with him because he was

---

[10] More information on Syria's Palestinian community and its treatment since conflict broke out is available in a Human Rights Watch report: http://www.hrw.org/en/node/126090/section/5

an Assad-supporter, he was on good terms with his cousin, who was born in Germany and lived near Frankfurt. Through his meagre financial reserves and some help from his cousin, he booked a flight to Khartoum, Sudan, and paid smugglers 1,400 dollars to bring him from Khartoum to Zuwara, a town on Libya's northwest coast. There, he paid another 800 dollars to cross the Mediterranean Sea.

The trip from Khartoum to Zuwara lasted about two weeks. Akil said they were the most difficult weeks of his life. Smugglers seated him and dozens of others on the open bed of a pickup truck to cross the desert into Libya, and forbade anyone from carrying any baggage. Water was scarce, and Sudanese soldiers robbed them on their way out of the country. Akil lost 500 dollars, but managed to keep the money he had hidden well. In Libya, the conditions he faced during stopovers were horrendous. He slept on floors in barren buildings and told me that the food usually given to him was a sort of grain porridge with no condiments that was so low in nutritional value that no amount of it would satiate him. But he was even privileged to receive that.

As Akil recalled his memory of one particular multi-day stopover at a farm, his eyes watered. He and some fellow Syrians were housed in a windowless room inside a building, and were given the porridge he hated. One night, he encountered an African woman with a child who looked dangerously thin and weak. He approached them, and found out that they hadn't eaten in days – the smugglers didn't give them any food at all. Akil asked the farm owner to give them food, but the farmer brushed him off, saying that the blacks didn't need to eat. Shocked, Akil set out to steal food from the farmer and give it to the Africans, which he discovered were housed in a foul-smelling chicken coop at the edge of the farm grounds. With his voice cracking, Akil told me that the farmer soon noticed that someone was stealing food, and angrily demanded to know who it was. Akil didn't admit it was him, no one else took responsibility, and to his horror, the farmer entered the chicken coop with a leather belt and furiously whipped the Africans simply out of suspicion.

When Akil finally reached Zuwara, he was exhausted. The weather wasn't good enough to attempt a crossing when he arrived, so he waited along with hundreds of other migrants in the hands of the same smuggling ring. Two boats departed shortly before Akil did, but returned due to engine problems. When it was Akil's turn, he and over 400 others waded waist-deep into the sea and boarded rafts that brought them to a large wooden boat further out. The deck was packed with migrants sitting between each others' legs, the engine came alive, and the boat set out on its final voyage. As the boat gathered speed, a cold wind blew through Akil's wet clothes, and he huddled together with others around him to try to keep as warm as possible.

Akil's boat travelled two days and two nights, during which time many migrants got seasick and vomited. Akil was spared seasickness, but he couldn't sleep, and spent the long hours keeping an eye on the horizon. During the second night, they approached a group of oil rigs in the distance, but never reached them. Suddenly, in the middle of the night, the engine stopped. They were stranded on the high seas, and called for help with a satellite phone. At 6 o'clock in the morning, a large container ship appeared on the horizon, heading towards them. The ship slowed as it approached the boat, and finally stopped right next to it. Everyone was overjoyed – the presence of the giant ship towering above them guaranteed their rescue, which came six hours later in the form of an Italian Coast Guard vessel.

While they were waiting for the Coast Guard to arrive, a scuffle broke out when the smuggler who had driven the boat joined the migrants on deck and told them to tell the Italian authorities that there was no smuggler onboard; that instead, they had all taken turns driving. Worried about the consequences, some of the migrants protested, and the smuggler threatened them with a knife. Someone on the container ship must have been watching and sent pictures to the Coast Guard, because when the Italians arrived, the smuggler was immediately identified and arrested.

The Coast Guard brought everyone to Augusta, two days after I had visited. They spent a night at a reception facility there and were transferred to a reception centre in Syracuse the next day. Some were given clothing, but not everyone; Akil wasn't, and he didn't even get the chance to take a shower. After a night in the centre, he walked out with a few other Syrians when the police wasn't looking, and wandered around Syracuse trying to find a place to change dollars into Euros and buy new clothes. He managed to find a clothing store that would accept dollars and the friendly owner even helped them change the rest of their money into Euros, and explained how to get to Catania in order to catch a train or coach leaving Sicily.

*\*\*\**

## From Milan to the Inner Wall

After 18 and 1/2 hours, the coach finally reached Milan at 14:30 the next day. Akil wanted to proceed to Germany immediately, but had no money left, and needed to retrieve a few hundred Euros his cousin sent him through Western Union before he could continue his journey. Unfortunately, his cousin didn't state his name exactly the same way it was written on his passport, and the Western Union agent at Milan's central train station refused to disburse the money until the sender corrected it. In the time it took to fix the mistake, it became too late for Akil to catch the last connection of the day to Germany. He had to stay the night in Milan, but he wouldn't be homeless.

In October 2013, Milan's municipal government set up a refugee support service in collaboration with local NGOs which provides general assistance to newly arrived refugees inside Milan's central train station, as well as medical assistance, clothing, showers, dormitory and canteen facilities outside the station. The Red Cross has also been involved in providing assistance since January 2015. This support, combined with Milan's geographical location and well-connected railway network to other parts of Europe, makes the city a natural gateway for refugees seeking to leave Italy. I left Akil with the social workers, who were receiving the others who travelled with us on the coach, knowing he would be in good hands, and headed home.

Akil made his way to the Brenner the next day. He arrived in the evening, in time to catch the 8 o'clock train to Munich. Four days after he arrived in Augusta. Less than 2 hours away from the German border. He was unlucky. Four Austrian police officers got on the train at the Brenner that evening. Northern Europe's gatekeepers at work, because people like Akil, from Yarmouk in Syria, which was overrun by Islamic State militants who beheaded residents while Akil was at sea, aren't welcome. Because Akil should not be allowed to reach his cousin in Germany, ready to help him emotionally and financially, but should rather fend for himself in Italy, among thousands of others forced to stay there.

Thankfully, an Egyptian man who cleans trains at the Brenner was very kind and let Akil spend the night in his company's office, which has a rest area complete with a bed located in a wing of the train station. I went to the Brenner myself the next day, and met Akil in the waiting room. He was in high spirits despite the setbacks, and looked relatively well rested. Hakim had been there the day before, and had given him a heavier jacket and new shoes, which definitely helped his overall appearance as well. When the 12 o'clock train arrived, we said goodbye hastily, not knowing whether he would make it this time, and he hurried onboard undetected.

I spent the whole day at the Brenner wondering whether he had been caught further down the line and whether he would be brought back to the Brenner like so many others, but he wasn't. In the late evening, I received a text from him: he was in Frankfurt, with his cousin. His gruelling journey was over. He made it.

# Part 4: Politics, Paradoxes and Solutions

## The besieged Inner Wall

In the weeks following my visit to Sicily, thousands of new migrants arrived. Most were rescued by the Italian Coast Guard, some were found by vessels belonging to the EU's Triton mission, and even cargo ships brought refugees to safety. Springtime's better weather allowed for record numbers of departures from Libya's shores. However, not everyone made it across the Mediterranean. Over 800 migrants lost their lives when their boat capsized while being rescued, in a tragedy that received major international media coverage and prompted the EU to discuss further measures to address the issue.

As part of the wave of new arrivals headed north, Bolzano and the Brenner became swamped with refugees kicked off of Munich-bound international trains. Local newspapers regularly reported about days in which 100 or more migrants arrived at Bolzano's train station, and concerned local residents spontaneously organized themselves to provide assistance to refugees well before NGOs mobilized their resources. Practically all the migrants continued their trips on regional trains to the Brenner after being handed the usual invitation to regularize their status by Italian police, creating chaotic scenes at the border. As migrants accumulated at the Brenner each day, the tri-national patrols stepping off trains there no longer left the platform unattended to chat or get a coffee as they had before. However, the sheer number of people trying to get on trains often resulted in comical cat-and-mouse chases that would only stop some of them. Hopelessly outnumbered police officers would block access to a few doors, only to run after migrants getting on the train further up or down the platform, leaving the previously guarded doors open to others.

As the flow of migrants became unmanageable, Italian police became less and less concerned about stopping them, and openly called for the trilateral patrols to end and the Dublin Regulation to be abolished[11]. Migrants at the Brenner told me that Italian police officers in Bolzano advised them how to get to the Brenner in order to proceed to Germany, and I witnessed an Italian police officer personally tell migrants at the Brenner to board the last train wagon, so that his Austrian colleague at the front wouldn't see them. But even some Austrian officers softened their stance when faced with the masses of defenceless women, children and teenagers stuck at the border with looks of fear and desperation on their faces. While chatting with some volunteers on the platform, a friendly older Austrian policeman told us that he would join us after he retires.

Despite the Italian police's lax approach, and a growing moral conscience among some of their

---

[11] Statements made by the police union's president in the "Alto Adige" local newspaper.

northern colleagues, it was still more difficult to board trains to Munich than before. Unchecked 8 o'clock trains became less common, and the trilateral patrols were soon joined by a small team of Italian police officers on the platform each time the international train arrived. As a result, migrants increasingly used Austrian regional trains, despite the risk of getting sent back if found en route to (or in) Innsbruck.

One particularly disturbing consequence of the increasingly difficult passage to Germany by train was to drive refugees in the hands of unscrupulous smugglers – with sometimes terrible results. The story of four Syrian women, a mother with her teenage daughter and two sisters in their 20s, should be a clear wake-up call that the Dublin Regulation must go. The mother and daughter wanted to go to Denmark, while the sisters' destination was Sweden. In Milan, an Eastern European man with what sounded like a Russian accent offered to drive them to Denmark in his car for 1,400 Euros. They departed at night, and crossed the Brenner at around 3 A.M. Shortly after crossing the border, the smuggler left the motorway, drove up a remote mountain road and stopped. He threatened them with a knife, robbed them of all their money and possessions, including their mobile phones, and drove off. The terrified women walked along the road back to the motorway, where they found an SOS telephone to call for help. The Austrian police arrived, quickly realized the women were in the country illegally, and brought them back to the Brenner, where Hakim found them in tears later that morning.

I could go on and on with more examples of desperation and determination, misfortune and good luck. The list of people who are seeking to leave Italy or have already left for a better future elsewhere in Europe is long and growing. Northern Europe's efforts to keep them out are not only failing, but creating dangerous side-effects that help no one but opportunistic criminals. To those who have crossed deserts and seas to flee conflict and deprivation, border patrols are merely another obstacle to overcome en route to a better future. Making life difficult for them at the Brenner will only delay their arrival, not prevent it.

\*\*\*

## The consequences of closed borders

Immigration hardliners in northern Europe regularly complain about the porous nature of internal EU borders, and frequently call for the reintroduction of pre-Schengen border controls in order to keep migrants out. It is assumed that closed borders will deter migrants, convincing them to stay in the southern European countries they want to leave. This hypothesis could be directly tested from 26 May to 15 June 2015, when Germany suspended Schengen for three weeks, supposedly to identify potential terrorists and violent demonstrators seeking to disrupt the 2015 G7 summit, which was held in a luxury hotel in Bavaria on 7-8 June. The temporary reintroduction of border controls in Germany had a direct impact on the flow of refugees trying to head north via the Brenner, with dramatic consequences.

In response to the anticipated pile-up of refugees unable to reach Germany on international trains to Munich as before, Austria reinforced its police presence at the Brenner and on trains transiting Austria. Italy was requested to implement similar measures, which it did by deploying special police and Carabinieri brigades to the Brenner in order to prevent migrants from boarding trains to Munich. From one day to the next, the Brenner was essentially militarized. The new situation shocked me at first sight. Groups of 10-15 muscular, intimidating men wearing berets, black vests and dark sunglasses now menacingly patrolled the platforms, and were initially joined by equally large numbers of Austrian police officers. On one occasion, over 30 policemen kept a watchful eye on roughly 100 frightened refugees who didn't even try to get onboard a train to Munich, while passengers inside watched the scene apprehensively from their windows.

The new police and Carabinieri brigades didn't only look threatening, but actually used force more than once on migrants taken off of trains or returned from Austria who refused to be fingerprinted. In one incident, a volunteer brought a returnee with a sprained wrist to the hospital after he claimed to have been physically forced to provide his fingerprints against his will, and used as an example to intimidate others who were also refusing to cooperate. I saw the man wearing a cast the next day, and spoke to another refugee who had had a similar experience, with swollen wrists to prove it. Sadly, the legality of such methods is unclear, and certainly difficult to challenge. Recently published EU guidelines on fingerprinting even recommend coercive measures to be carried out if a "data-subject" doesn't cooperate.[12]

To make matters worse for migrants at the Brenner, the special police forces deployed there had very little knowledge of border laws. On one occasion, they refused to let a Tunisian man board a train, although he had a valid Italian residence permit and his passport with him, which entitled him to travel within the Schengen area as a tourist for up to 90 days. The visibly uncertain police officers dealing with him told him that he needed to have a German employment contract or written job offer with him to cross the border. They didn't consult anyone or any documents, apparently preferring to invent a plausible reason to keep him off the train, preventing him from visiting his cousin in Munich.

Police checks across the border in Austria intensified as well, leading to a record number of returns – 715 in the first two weeks of June alone. Migrants who nevertheless somehow managed to get all the way to

---

[12] More information available at:
http://www.statewatch.org/analyses/no-270-fingerprinting-migrants-coercive-measures.pdf

the German border faced a dangerous trap. I met two Eritreans at the Brenner who had been kicked off a Munich-bound train by German police in Rosenheim, the first stop after the border, and handed over to Austrian police, which returned them to the Brenner without further ado. They were both fingerprinted in Rosenheim and given documents they didn't understand, which they asked me to explain. In the most legalistic, bureaucratic German imaginable, the "affected parties" were informed that they would be deported from Germany for having entered the country illegally, and that a two year entry ban was issued against them. German police apparently decided to use the opportunity of enhanced border controls to put a definite end to the dreams of anyone who didn't know they had to say the magic word "asylum" in order to be considered a refugee, rather than a criminal.

Despite the border controls and forced fingerprinting, most migrants refused to stay in Italy. An exasperated Palestinian man from the Gaza strip I spoke to even asked me how he could return to Gaza, since he simply could not envision a future for himself in Italy. Many others decided to keep trying to get on trains until they made it, despite the impossible odds and risks of getting caught. The rapidly accumulating number of people stuck at the Brenner finally prompted emergency humanitarian action to be taken, when 120 people were stuck at the station after the last train had left without them. Volontarius received cots from Italy's disaster relief agency and we put them in two large, empty apartments located atop a former lamp store that we had previously moved into from the small apartment used at the beginning of the year. The beds were hastily placed in every corner of the building, despite the poor condition of the empty apartments, which had fallen into disrepair over the course of 10 years of disuse.

The first night that the refugees stayed in the facility was literally a nightmare. In the early morning hours, a sewage pipe leading to one of the upstairs toilets broke, partially flooding the ground floor, where refugees were also sleeping. The local fire brigade was called to fix the pipe, and clean-up efforts lasted well into the next day. Since the empty upstairs apartments had no lighting, a chain of Christmas lights from a nearby town were brought in to illuminate the premises. Chaotic scenes literally a few hundred meters from the Austrian border, demarcating the boundary of consequences Austria and Germany didn't want to deal with.

Despite the poor conditions, most migrants, having nowhere else to go, wanted to stay the next night as well. I was asked to do night shifts at the facility as a temporary staff member, which I did starting the following day. By then, most of the migrants had left – some to find another route to Germany, some to try their luck on regional trains to Innsbruck, and a few were willing to seek shelter elsewhere in Italy while they waited for the border to reopen. Practically no one even thought of giving up, as Bavaria's State Minister for Labour, Social Affairs, Family and Integration had publicly hoped. In a press conference on the issue, she plainly stated: "We hope that when the border reopens, many of them [the refugees] will have decided to apply for asylum in other countries."[13]

In the days that followed, more and more refugees accumulated at the Brenner who refused to leave until they were able to reach Germany. Many attempted to reach Innsbruck on regional trains, but practically everyone was returned. As our facility had limited space, which we prioritized for new arrivals, people started sleeping in the train station's small waiting room and snack room. When they became full of long-term guests, some refugees occupied an empty train company storage room on one of the platforms. Towards the end of the border closure, around 100 young men, women and children were constantly present at the Brenner, living in appalling conditions our team didn't have the resources to improve beyond free food rations, covers and pain killers.

By the end of the first day after Germany's borders reopened, all the refugees stuck at the Brenner disappeared. Italian special police forces remained stationed at the border until the end of the month, but their attitude had softened over the course of the three weeks they had seen the increasing misery around them. After the end of the border closure, they were completely passive, sometimes even encouraging

---

[13] Full details (in Italian) available at:
http://altoadige.gelocal.it/bolzano/cronaca/2015/05/28/news/la-baviera-per-noi-stop-ai-profughi-1.11513618?ref=search

refugees to board trains to Munich. As a result, hundreds of refugees crossed the Brenner in the days and weeks that followed.

I recognized the faces of some of the migrants who had been stranded during the border closure; many more recognized me. Their determination to reach family members, friends and a better life in northern Europe was as strong as ever. There was no stopping them. All the efforts to keep them out – with the associated financial and humanitarian cost – achieved nothing but a delay in their arrival. Patience, perseverance and a basic sense of humanity prevailed over policies and procedures.

***

## Fallacies and false assumptions

In the aftermath of the well-documented migrant boat tragedy that killed over 800 people in April 2015, European politicians quickly found a scapegoat for the wider immigration issue: smugglers. French President François Hollande called smugglers "terrorists", while Italian Prime Minister Matteo Renzi referred to them as "slave-holders". In an extraordinary EU summit that was held less than a week after the incident, European leaders called for the targeted identification, capture and destruction of vessels before they are used by smugglers in order to stem the flow of migrants.

The overwhelming focus on and demonization of smugglers is an obvious political strategy, but one that is incredibly far removed from the reality of the situation. The image of the smuggler as an evil criminal packing defenceless Africans into crowded boats like slave traders in colonial times is an easy one to sell to the public, and destroying their boats is a simple and seemingly convincing answer to irregular immigration: sink boats and punish smugglers, and the problem will go away. Sadly, the consequences of this approach only cause refugees to suffer even more than they already do, and will not stop the flow of migrants to Europe. Smugglers are not slave traders or terrorists, they don't force anyone to cross the Mediterranean; migrants are desperate to get on their boats and pay large sums of money to be let onboard. Media reports about smugglers pushing migrants out to sea in poor weather conditions and threatening those who resist rarely explain that such incidents are the result of smugglers' crude operational methods, profit maximization and lack of sympathy, not an overall coercion. Destroying their boats will only make the trip more expensive and more dangerous, as more people will be packed on fewer, smaller and likely damaged boats and rafts that can hardly withstand rough seas.

As long as there are no legal ways for asylum-seekers to reach Europe, there will be a market for smuggling. Smugglers are the only people providing a service that is in very high demand, which is why they can charge exorbitant prices while offering the absolute minimum level of comfort and safety imaginable. Europe needs to understand and acknowledge that smugglers are businessmen, ruthless opportunistic businessmen to be sure, who squeeze as much money from migrants as they can, and take advantage of their desperation. But they are not terrorists, not slave traders and not the root cause of immigration.

Besides the vilification of smugglers, another major fallacy in the debate about how to stop the flow of migrants crossing the Mediterranean is focusing on North African countries, particularly Libya. Following the April 2015 tragedy, politicians of all colours pointed to Libya's dysfunctional political landscape, with its two semi-official governments and several other conflicting groups, and declared that Libya's chaotic circumstances were causing people to flee. Therefore, the solution would be to stabilize the country in one way or another. No one bothered to check whether Libyans themselves were actually fleeing their own country or not. Interestingly, only the fewest are. Out of the 663,990 asylum-seekers present in Europe in 2014, only 3,560 were Libyan nationals[14] – 0.5% of the total. The reality is that migrants leaving Libya are from everywhere except Libya. Stabilizing the country would probably lead to an EU-financed crackdown against irregular migrants, as occurred towards the end of the Gaddafi

---

[14] Eurostat [migr_asyappctza] data

118

regime and is still underway in Morocco[15], but it won't make migrants disappear. Syrians, Eritreans, Somalis, Nigerians, Ghanaians and Gambians will find other routes to Europe until the problems in their home countries are resolved – or at least not exacerbated by misguided development aid programmes.

A good example of how the EU is actually encouraging immigration through actions intended to reduce it is precisely the development aid granted to Eritrea, one of the most corrupt, oppressive regimes in the world, which its residents are fleeing in droves. Its president, Isaias Afwerki, has ruled the country with a heavy hand since 1991. All of the country's private news outlets were closed down in 2001, journalists were arrested (most of whom have since died in prison camps) and it has been ranked last place worldwide in Reporters Without Borders' press freedom index for the eighth consecutive year, right after North Korea. A UN Human Rights Council report published in June 2015 described "systemic, widespread and gross human rights violations" including mass surveillance, forced labour and torture, which may even amount to crimes against humanity.[16] Despite this troubling reality, the EU not only continues to provide development aid money, but even tripled the amount to be granted

---

[15] Details available at:
http://www.thelocal.es/20150211/morocco-crackdown-continues-at-spains-border
[16] UN Press Release with link to full report:
http://www.ohchr.org/EN/NewsEvents/Pages/DisplayNews.aspx?NewsID=16054&LangID=E

between 2015 and 2020 – 312 million Euros in total – compared to what was spent on the dictatorship in 2010-2015. An Italian delegation that visited Eritrea in March 2015 only received vague assurances from the government that it would conduct democratic reforms "in its own way" over the next few years.[17] Europe's diplomacy is incredibly naïve to think that these kinds of regimes won't use aid money to further oppress their own people and thus convince even more of them to leave.

The third major fallacy of Europe's irregular immigration situation that resurfaced in the aftermath of the tragedy is that the EU institutions are responsible for the lack of resources and willingness to tackle the issue. National European politicians, as well as the wider public, are quick to blame shortfalls on an abstract notion of "Brussels" without recognizing that the EU has very limited competences in the field of migration. It is largely up to the member states to agree on measures, finance and staff them. Frontex, the oft-cited EU border agency, has no Coast Guard ships, patrol vehicles or border guards of its own, but rather coordinates joint operations (such as Triton) using individual member states' equipment and staff. Meanwhile, the European Commission can only propose legislation, and does, but Europe's

---

[17] See Reporters Without Borders report:
http://en.rsf.org/erythree-eu-plans-to-provide-eritrea-s-28-04-2015,47814.html

governments oppose any suggestions that might be too unpopular with their electorates. At the EU summit that followed the migrant shipwreck, European Commission President Jean-Claude Juncker pushed for legal immigration channels and more resettlement programmes, but both proposals were rejected by Europe's heads of state.

\*\*\*

## Trickery in Dublin's shadow

Irregular migration is a complex issue with a multitude of problems that are difficult to solve, but northern Europe's approach to the matter is making things worse than they need to be. Northern Europe's lack of solidarity with southern Europe and insistence on the Dublin Regulation is creating a situation that puts an unfair strain on Europe's southern frontier and dooms refugees to misery unless they circumvent the rules. It is absurd to expect migrants who have support in other countries to stay in the first country they set foot in. It is absurd to let them accumulate in countries suffering from chronically high unemployment, where they can only hope to be exploited on the black labour market. And it is naïve to think that southern European governments won't deal with the situation their own way behind northern Europeans' backs, regardless of what has been agreed on paper in Brussels.

Northern Europe's attempts to isolate itself from the refugee crisis in the Mediterranean have certainly led to legally questionable practices in southern European countries aiming to limit the burden imposed on them because of their geographic location. The consistently high number of non-fingerprinted refugees arriving at the Brenner just days after arriving in Sicily is a case in point. Authorities at initial reception centres don't hinder new arrivals from leaving before they are fingerprinted, and implicitly encourage the departure of migrants most likely to obtain asylum elsewhere. A group of Eritreans I met at the Brenner told me that in the reception centre they were taken to after arriving in Sicily, Nigerians and Ghanaians were fingerprinted immediately, while Syrians, Eritreans and Somalis were told they would be fingerprinted in a few days' time if they stayed. Unsurprisingly, no one did.

At the same time, the legality of northern Europe's methods is questionable as well. The tri-national patrols on Munich-bound trains likely violate the Schengen Borders Code, which regulates how Europe's internal borders are to be managed. According to Article 20 of the Schengen Borders Code, *"Internal borders may be crossed at any point without a border check on persons, irrespective of their nationality, being carried out."*[18] However, police activities that *"do not have an effect equivalent to border checks"* are permitted, as long as they *"do not have border control as an objective, are based on general police information*

---

[18] Article 20, Schengen Borders Code

*and experience regarding possible threats to public security and aim, in particular, to combat cross-border crime, are devised and executed in a manner clearly distinct from systematic checks on persons at the external borders, and are carried out on the basis of spot-checks".*[19]

Police officers who look for dark-skinned people on trains in order to check their documents are conducting activities that are hardly distinct from systematic checks. Their daily presence on trains heading north also amounts to more than spot-checks, but the mystery of the unchecked 8 o'clock train may be precisely the answer to this legal constraint. It would be very difficult to argue that checking every train every day is not more than spot-checking, but leaving one per day unchecked still leaves room for a creative interpretation of Schengen rules.

Another example of how southern and northern European countries work against each other using (or ignoring) mechanisms designed to foster cooperation is the way in which so-called Dublin transfers are handled. Migrants who do not qualify to seek asylum in a particular country because it can be proven that they first arrived in a different country, usually due to fingerprints entered in the EURODAC database, can be returned as a "Dublin case". In order to return the migrant to the country in which he or she first arrived, a request must be submitted to and accepted by the asylum authorities of the receiving country within 11

---

[19] Article 21, Schengen Borders Code

months (9 months for those who have already initiated an asylum application there).

Eurostat statistics from 2013 show that Germany, Sweden and Switzerland submitted the most requests, slightly over 52,000 in total.[20] Italy received by far the most requests, with over 15,500.[21] Interestingly, only 3,460 transfers were carried out[22] – perhaps after the majority of requests were allowed to expire so that a transfer could no longer take place. However, I have personally witnessed Dublin cases being let off unmarked Austrian police buses at the Brenner, at a roundabout right by the border at the edge of town, completely bypassing the formal return procedure.

In the meantime, Germany has resorted to the very same practices it has criticised Italy for. Faced with an especially large influx of refugees in the first half of 2015, German police was no longer able (or willing) to register all new arrivals immediately, and simply told some of them to present themselves at the nearest immigration office to have their fingerprints taken there. In a letter addressed to German Interior Minister Thomas de Maizière, the Vice President of Germany's police union alerted him that between 250 and 300 irregular entries are not processed on a daily basis at a single border post in south-east Germany due to a lack of resources.[23] Although the issue has been known for

---

[20] Eurostat [migr_dubro] data
[21] Eurostat [migr_dubri] data
[22] Eurostat [migr_dubti] data
[23] As reported in *Der Spiegel* 29/2015, p. 47-48

some time, no measures have been enacted. According to *Der Spiegel*, the Interior Ministry has refused to confirm that there are any such difficulties.

The EU's credibility is seriously at risk if European countries resort to clever tactics to deal with migration. It is truly regrettable that EU member states try to outsmart each other and the regulations they've agreed on together because they do not want to assume responsibility for a common challenge. Rather than cooperate to solve the issue, they secretly work against each other. At the end, it is the most vulnerable who suffer the consequences. Refugees are ping-ponged across the Brenner because of Europe's lack of collaboration and particularly because of northern Europe's lack of solidarity with its southern neighbours.

The Dublin Regulation, and the walls it has erected within Europe, goes plainly against the principle of free movement that the EU holds so dear. The hypocrisy of forbidding refugees from choosing where to live in exile while celebrating Schengen as one of Europe's primary achievements is shameful. While Europeans can cross borders freely, refugees are humiliatingly picked out and kicked off of trains, returned against their will, and left to the mercy of smugglers without a hint of compassion. This indifference is especially disturbing in the face of grand statements about human rights that are regularly heard from European leaders. If we really care about human rights in the world, let us start by treating refugees as victims, not criminals.

***

## Answers to northern European concerns

While I firmly believe that the Dublin Regulation should be abolished, I understand that northern Europeans' concerns must be taken seriously. The main fear is that northern European countries would be flooded with migrants if Dublin weren't in place, which is an understandable worry. Finding accommodation for refugees isn't easy, and more migrants cost more money (in the short term, since today's migrant is tomorrow's taxpayer). However, the reality is that migrants who want to reach northern Europe already do. In 2014, over 170,000 migrants came to Italy by sea, on top of close to 43,000 who arrived in 2013[24]. However, according to Eurostat statistics, Germany has by far the most pending asylum applications in Europe, with well over 200,000 at the end of 2014.[25] Sweden is in second place, with over 50,000 applications, while Italy is only third, with slightly less than 50,000.[26]

Of course, in addition to those who have been accepted into northern European asylum procedures, there are the so-called Dublin cases mentioned above. But the numbers of transfers are far smaller than the overall totals. Apart from allowing a few thousand extra

---

[24] IOM data available at: http://www.iom.int/news/migrant-arrivals-sea-italy-top-170000-2014
[25] Eurostat *Data in focus* 3/2015
[26] Same source

migrants to stay in the main northern European receiving countries, and far less in smaller states, not much in terms of numbers would change if the Dublin Regulation were to be abolished. Indeed, the total influx might even recede after a possible initial spike. Reducing the pressure on southern European countries' reception systems would allow them to tackle their backlog of asylum applications, thus freeing up space in overcrowded reception centres and improving conditions for refugees inside them. Many migrants I spoke to in Sicily and at the Brenner actually liked Italy and would have liked to stay, but were frustrated by long waiting times and poor reception conditions.

In order to further reassure northern Europeans, annual quota limits could be introduced, which would divert refugees to other countries if a certain maximum number is reached in any individual country. Unlike other quota proposals that have been floated in Brussels, this would not set a number that every country must fulfil, but rather act as a relief mechanism in case of a particularly large influx to a specific country. In order to avoid separating families, only those who do not have particular ties to a destination country should be relocated. In order to support relocations to countries in Eastern Europe, which have relatively few asylum-seekers but also limited means to accommodate them, a European fund could be established to finance reception centres and related expenses. If the EU can set aside billions of Euros to bail out indebted member states, it should be able to collect a few hundred million to help pay for refugee accommodation.

Another often-heard northern European concern is that allowing migrants to roam freely around Europe would cause an unmanageable influx of unemployed refugees currently located in southern Europe. Interestingly, the fact that there are many times more unemployed southern Europeans who can freely move to northern European countries doesn't seem to be a problem, because it isn't. Once again, the perceived scale of migration is far greater than the reality. Of course, there will be some low-skilled migrants with little education or training who will find it difficult to find a job. But rather than grudgingly pay social welfare to these people, northern European governments – which have many more resources and better organized educational institutions than southern European ones – should invest in them. Practically every migrant I have met was eager to work and eager to learn. Countries with well-established apprenticeship programmes like Germany could benefit tremendously from such highly motivated individuals if they were willing to finance their training.

Yet another reason for resistance to new migrants in northern Europe is the argument that it is already full of migrants who are unwilling or unable to integrate into society. These worries are legitimate, as there are real problems with alienated, sometimes radicalized youths with so-called "migratory backgrounds" immersed in dangerous sub-cultures plagued by unemployment.

However, these youths are usually not migrants at all, but rather the disillusioned children and grandchildren of migrant workers who came before anyone even spoke of integration. There is a fundamental difference between someone who has risked their life for a better future today and someone who was born into the socially marginalized, low-income household of yesteryear's guest workers.

Finally, a look at demographic trends in Europe should make it clear that migration is the only way European countries can sustain their economies and welfare systems in the long term. The EU's fertility rate (the number of live births per woman) has been in decline for decades; in 2013, it was 1.55[27] – a rate of 2.1 is considered to be the minimum required to keep population size constant in the absence of migration. Fertility rates in all European countries are below the minimum replacement level, not only in southern Europe. Germany's fertility rate in 2013 was 1.39, Switzerland's was 1.52, Sweden's was 1.89 and Denmark's was 1.67.[28] At the same time, life expectancy is rising across the EU. Over the past 50 years, life expectancy at birth has increased by about 10 years.[29] Clearly, migration is the only way to ensure that pensions can still be paid and economies don't shrink in

---

[27] Eurostat [demo_find] data (provisional as of July 2015)
[28] Eurostat [demo_find] data
[29] Eurostat report available at:
http://ec.europa.eu/eurostat/statistics-explained/index.php/Mortality_and_life_expectancy_statistics

the not too distant future. Expecting this population deficit to be corrected by an influx of pre-selected scientists with PhDs in Astrophysics, as discussions about highly qualified migrants sometimes suggest, is unrealistic.

*** 

## Unfounded fears and unrecognised opportunities

A common slogan in Germany is that it can't be the world's welfare office. This statement reflects overall European sentiments about the wider issue of immigration beyond questions relating to the Dublin Regulation. There is an entrenched fear that if Europe relaxes its immigration laws, it would open the floodgates to millions of impoverished foreigners ready to create ethnic enclaves in Europe financed by taxpayers' money. Even many of those who support easing restrictions for "legitimate" asylum-seekers from war-torn countries like Syria simultaneously call for strictness with so-called "economic migrants".

There are several problems with these views. Firstly, the scale of migration is vastly overstated. Not everyone who lives a precarious life abroad wants to come to Europe. A look at the main countries of origin of irregular boat migrant arrivals over the past 5 years shows that with few exceptions, they come from the world's most dysfunctional countries: Syria, Eritrea, Afghanistan, Tunisia, Somalia, Nigeria, Palestinian

Territories, Mali, Gambia and Egypt. There are plenty more countries with large populations living in poverty and even conflict, but relatively few citizens of those countries venture to Europe despite their misery. Those who do emigrate, even from the most devastated nations, usually stay in neighbouring countries in the hope of returning as soon as conditions improve. In fact, over 86% of the world's refugees are hosted by developing countries, not industrialized ones.[30]

It is important to understand that the push factors resulting from war, repression and extreme poverty are stronger than the pull factors of a potentially bright future in Europe. It is usually a combination of factors that cause people to leave their countries, which is why the distinction between "real" refugees and economic migrants is often problematic. Most people leave their countries due to a multitude of political and economic reasons, and it is only in a handful of countries that those overlapping factors are serious enough to push significant numbers of people out across very long distances.

Of course, some people do come to Europe solely to find work, and may have unrealistic expectations of professional success. Some even come with illusions of incredible wealth easily available in Europe. These ideas are fuelled by the Western media, which is readily available and consumed in the developing world. While

---

[30] More worldwide refugee statistics available at:
http://www.unhcr.org.uk/about-us/key-facts-and-figures.html

the average European will implicitly understand that glossy images of celebrities and their expensive toys are only accessible to a tiny minority of people, those same images will have an entirely different effect on those who do not know the bigger picture. It is normal for people to dream, and to attach their hopes and desires to a better place.

How should Europe deal with the dreamers? My approach would be to let a controlled number of migrants enter Europe each year on temporary visas that would allow them to look for work, but with no right to claim benefits of any sort. If they find employment, they can stay, and if they don't they must return. That way, potential migrants can see for themselves what conditions are like and report those observations back to their friends and family members. There is a risk of absconding, but I believe that most people faced with homelessness in a foreign country would return home voluntarily. At the very least, such a programme could be tested as a pilot project, and discontinued if too many people disappear after they arrive.

Regardless of whether migrants arrive due to unbearable conditions in their home countries or simply unemployment, there is a pervasive fear of letting too many foreigners into Europe who will stay indefinitely. However, in reality, many migrants have no intention of staying in Europe permanently. Those who flee war and persecution may return home as soon as conflict in their country of origin ends or the political regime changes. Many of those who come for work simply want to earn enough money to be able to finance a house or education for their children back home. Remittances arguably even prevent further migration, since they are an important source of income for entire families in developing countries that have few other means to support themselves.

Allowing migrants to support their families from abroad doesn't only make sense from the standpoint of limiting the number of migrants arriving to Europe. It is also an alternative approach to traditional development aid which would bypass corrupt, oppressive governments. Already today, remittances account for a significant portion of external funds arriving in developing countries, and that amount is increasing exponentially. According to World Bank data, remittance flows were three times larger than official development assistance in 2013, and with the exception of China, remittances were also significantly higher than foreign direct investment to developing countries.[31] Some of the poorer developing countries in Sub-Saharan Africa absolutely depend on these funds. Remittances represented 24% of Lesotho's GDP, 20% of Gambia's, 19% of Liberia's and 11% of Senegal's economy in 2013.[32] Sadly, Sub-Saharan Africa is also the costliest region to which to send remittances, with average money transfer fees of over 11% in the third

---

[31] The World Bank Migration and Development Brief 23, p. 3
[32] Same source, p. 11

quarter of 2014.[33] The United Nations General Assembly recognized the importance of remittances and the need to lower transaction costs in a unanimously adopted declaration from October 2013.[34] Changing EU migration laws would help implement that declaration.

A more flexible immigration system would require the political courage to give more migrants the chance to pursue their dreams, but it wouldn't need to cost any welfare money at all. Indeed, in light of demographic trends, it could be presented as a boost to tax revenues permitting pensions to be funded. In fact, in many cases, migrants wouldn't even qualify for a full pension themselves due to lacking years of contributions. To further increase the public's acceptance of refugees, asylum-seekers who are physically able to work and do not have children to look after (the overwhelming majority) could be asked to perform socially useful tasks in communities where their reception centres are located, in exchange for some extra pocket money. These tasks could include picking up rubbish in parks, assisting in road construction and repairs, or assisting handicapped and elderly residents in local hospitals and retirement homes. If European governments don't want to ease restrictions on granting asylum-seekers full access to the labour market, the least they could do for both refugees and local communities is to offer them

---

[33] Same source, p. 14
[34] Full text available at:
http://www.un.org/ga/search/view_doc.asp?symbol=A/68/L.5

the chance to prove themselves useful rather than force them to be idle while waiting for their documents.

Changing the way migration is framed is admittedly not an easy task, and is unfortunately not one that is politically worth the effort for most elected officials, considering the fact that migrants have very limited voting rights, if any, in most countries. This is an issue that would need to be pushed by Europeans themselves. But despite the difficulties, I am optimistic that a lot can be done and also will be done out of sheer necessity in the years to come.

\*\*\*

## Public opinion: the key to better migration policies

Public opinion is both a fundamental requirement for, and the biggest obstacle to improving Europe's asylum and migration laws. The basis of democratic change is public opinion, and politicians pay attention to it closely, whether voters believe it or not. As things stand, Europeans don't have high opinions of non-EU immigrants. According to a Eurobarometer poll conducted in November 2014, 57% of Europeans have negative feelings about the immigration of people from outside the EU.[35] An overwhelming 82% of Europeans believe that additional measures should be taken to fight irregular immigration.[36] At the same time, 71% of

---

[35] QA11.2 Eurobarometer 82.3
[36] QA12 Eurobarometer 82.3

Europeans are in favour of a common European policy on migration.[37]

I believe that a lot of the negativity surrounding the issue is a natural human fear of the unknown, rather than an outright rejection of newcomers. A look at public opinion on the immigration of people from other EU member states reveals that a majority of Europeans are not against it: 52% of Europeans have positive feelings about the immigration of EU citizens, versus 41% who have negative feelings.[38] A Spaniard in Finland probably feels about as foreign as a Syrian in Italy, yet Europeans have come to accept people from very different cultures within the union more than those from outside. Racism is probably a factor, but I don't think it's the primary reason for this apparent contradiction. For most people, it is simply a lack of knowledge about the "outsiders". Europeans know more about each other, or think they know more about each other, than those outside of the "club".

Knowledge about other cultures leads to respect, and that in turn leads to acceptance. I encourage Europeans to not only inform themselves about the cultures that people arriving in Europe are coming from, but also to seek contact with them. Simply talking to migrants rather than only about them goes a long way towards better understanding who they are and why they are in Europe. At the end of the day,

---

[37] QA19.6 Eurobarometer 82.3
[38] QA11.1 Eurobarometer 82.3

migration is about people – each one has an individual story that goes far beyond a news headline or statistic. The look of desperation in the eyes of a refugee who isn't allowed to reach loved ones in another country speaks volumes about a situation that is fundamentally humanitarian in nature. Facts and numbers may not change minds, but emotions do. If enough people rethink their stance on the issue, politicians will react.

I also find it promising that a strong majority of Europeans is in favour of a common European approach to migration. Granted, this may include support for tougher measures at Europe's external borders, but Frontex isn't very popular, despite its focus on keeping irregular migrants out of Europe. I suspect that there is a desire for a more orderly and organized way of handling immigration, which translates into an instinctive anti-immigrant reaction among Europeans simply out of the fear of an uncontrolled wave of new arrivals. Indeed, support for a common European approach to migration is even high in northern and Eastern European countries that would likely receive more migrants as a result of a more even distribution of refugees: 74% in Ireland, 70% in Poland, and even 84% in Lithuania.[39]

Politicians need not fear the polls if they support EU-level measures to deal with the issue. Right-wing politicians are filling the void created by Europe's lack of a common approach with hateful rhetoric against

---

[39] QA19.6 Eurobarometer 82.3

migrants, but the desire for a better organized immigration system could also be satisfied with concrete plans for well-coordinated humanitarian action. Europe needs more courageous, outspoken politicians who change opinions rather than cede the floor to right-wingers willing to exploit the plight of the world's weakest. The public needs guidance and reassurance on matters as complex and controversial as immigration, and if no one is willing to offer explanations and solutions, fear and prejudice will prevail.

***

## Europe's forgotten legacy

Not too long ago, millions of displaced Europeans became refugees in the aftermath of World War II. Thousands more fled the Eastern Bloc during the Cold War. Some of these former refugees are still alive today, and many more live on as the memory of our parents and grandparents. Yet we fail to connect their experiences with the tragic stories of today's refugees. Their hardship is as distant as that of the boatloads of migrants crossing the Mediterranean. Memories are short, and need reminding.

In 1940, Hitler and Mussolini met at the Brenner on two occasions. The first meeting took place shortly before Italy formally entered World War II, and wartime collaboration was discussed. In the second encounter, Mussolini informed Hitler about the successes of his offensive in Africa. The same Africa that today's refugees are fleeing, via the former Italian colony of Libya, and mainly from former Italian Eritrea and former Italian Somaliland. History's clever revenge.

From 1943 to the end of the war, thousands of Italian Jews were deported to concentration camps in Central Europe by rail across the Brenner. Seventy years ago, it was a gateway of death. Today, it is a gateway of hope. The most vulnerable people of today are desperate to cross the same border that the most vulnerable people of yesterday were forced to cross. In the space of a single lifetime, Italy and Germany have gone from being the world's oppressors to beacons of hope for the world's oppressed. Europe has transformed itself from a continent of war and misery to a continent of peace and prosperity – a tremendous achievement, which is recognized precisely by those who turn to us for protection.

Let us not allow our present to blind us from our past, or the plight of those around us. Let us treat refugees with the same dignity and respect that we would have wished upon our parents and grandparents, and that we would wish upon ourselves, our children and grandchildren if forced to flee. Let us stop barring those in need of our help. They will arrive anyway. They will keep trying to get on the train to Munich until they make it. They will try until they finally manage to leave the Brenner train station's platform 7, Europe's purgatory, behind them.

# Acknowledgements

First and foremost, I would like to thank my parents for their unwavering support from the very beginning. Their constant feedback, valuable input and constructive criticism made this book possible. I am incredibly fortunate to have the parents I do.

I would like to thank Volontarius, particularly the team of tireless staff and volunteers at the Brenner, with whom I've shared some unforgettable experiences. This book is a tribute to the solidarity you practice, rather than preach.

Special thanks go to Judith Gleitze at Borderline-Europe, who provided me with very useful information and tips for my trip to Sicily. I would not have been much more than a tourist if she hadn't pointed me in the right direction.

Thanks also to all the staff at the International Organization for Migration (IOM) Country Office for Austria, my former colleagues, who showed great enthusiasm for my project and gave me some impulses for the content of this book.

I would like to thank the journalist and writer Norbert Mappes-Niediek for making my book first known to the public in a newspaper article, and for trying to help me find a publisher.

Last, but far from least, I thank all of the migrants who I had the pleasure of meeting while writing this book. Their remarkable stories have touched me and inspired me. This book wouldn't even say half as much without them.

# About the Author

Marco Funk holds a Bachelor's degree in Political Science (International Relations) from the University of Central Florida and a Master's degree in European Affairs from Sciences Po Paris. He has gained professional experience at the Organization for Security and Co-operation in Europe (OSCE), EU Agency for Fundamental Rights and International Organization for Migration (IOM). He maintains a blog on European politics (europainmundo.blogactiv.eu) and is particularly interested in migration and human rights issues.

69389911R00087

Made in the USA
Middletown, DE
06 April 2018